Africana Womanist Literary Theory

Other Works by the Author

Africana Womanism: Reclaiming Ourselves
(Bedford, 1993—1st edition; 1997—3rd revised edition)

Emmett Till: The Sacrificial Lamb of the Civil Rights Movement
(Bedford, 1994—1 edition; 2000—3rd revised edition)

Toni Morrison, co-author with Wilfred D. Samuels
(Prentice Hall, 1990)

American Prose Library, Inc., an interview on Africana Womanism
with the author by Kay Bonetti (1995)

Unearthing Emmett Till: Passion for Truth
(a film script to be produced by the author and Barry Morrow,
Oscar Award-Winning writer for *Rain Man*)

Forthcoming

Contemporary Africana Theory and Thought:
A Guide to Africana Studies (2004)

Soul Mates (A novel)

Africana Womanist Literary Theory

A Sequel to
AfricanaWomanism: Reclaiming Ourselves

Clenora Hudson-Weems

Africa World Press, Inc.

P.O. Box 1892   P.O. Box 48
Trenton, NJ 08607   Asmara, ERITREA

Africa World Press, Inc.

P.O. Box 1892
Trenton, NJ 08607

P.O. Box 48
Asmara, ERITREA

Copyright: © 2004 Clenora Hudson-Weems
First Printing 2004

Cover and book design: Roger Dormann

Library of Congress Cataloging-in-Publication Data

Hudson-Weems, Clenora.
  Africana womanist literary theory / by Clenora Hudson-Weems.
    p. cm.
  ISBN 1-59221-055-4 (cloth) -- ISBN 1-59221-056-2 (pbk.)
  1. American literature--African American authors--History and criticism--Theory, etc. 2. American literature--Women authors--History and criticism--Theory, etc. 3. African literature (English)--Women authors--History and criticism--Theory, etc. 4. African American women--Intellectual life. 5. Feminism and literature--United States. 6. Women and literature--United States. 7. Women--Africa--Intellectual life. 8. Feminism and literature--Africa. 9. Women and literature--Africa. 10. Feminist literary criticism. 11. Sex role in literature. 12. Feminism in literature. 13. Women in literature. I. Title.

  PS153.N5H838 2004
  810.9'9287'08996073--dc22

                                      2004005427

AFRICANA WOMANISM

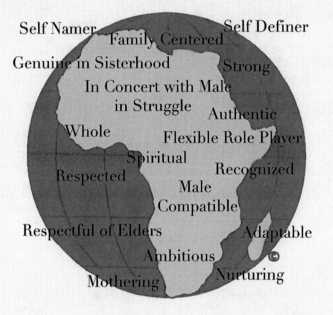

Self Namer
Self Definer
Family Centered
Genuine in Sisterhood
Strong
In Concert with Male
in Struggle
Authentic
Whole
Flexible Role Player
Spiritual
Respected
Recognized
Male
Compatible
Respectful of Elders
Adaptable
Ambitious
Mothering
Nurturing

FROM *AFRICANA WOMANISM: RECLAIMING OURSELVES*

Contents

Dedication

To God, the creator, who informs me, and to my strong, authentic Africana family: my loving mother, Mary, a model Africana womanist; my passionate daughter, Neimah, who reminds me constantly to be humble, gentle, and accurate; my husband and soul mate, Robert, who supports my life and dreams; my siblings, Juanita, Tara and Lee, who are always there for me; and my beloved late father, Matthew, and late brothers, Tommie and McCray, whom I shall never forget and who are on my mind daily. I miss you greatly. I also dedicate this book to my in-laws: my mother-in-law, Delores; my father-in-law, Robert, Sr.; my sisters-in-law, Delores and Donna. Moreover, I dedicate this book to all of my other beautiful family members, my cousins, nieces and nephews. Finally, I dedicate this book to my extended family: my colleagues, who inspire me through our endless dialogues, and my friends and supporters, who believe in me. We shall never give up on us. I love you all.

Foreword

Two of the most significant challenges for American higher education over the last three and an half decades have emerged from the Africana (Black) and Women's Studies movements. Africana Studies (Black Studies) began as a field of study in the 1960s in the wake of the civil rights movement and in the midst of pervasive campus unrest. Students were confronted with an absence or a distortion of the authentic Africana experience in the higher education curricula and a sense of cultural alienation generated by the predominantly white colleges and universities they entered. They fought for inclusion in the Academy of the experiences of Africana people. Women's Studies, following on the heels of the Black (Africana) Studies movement, sought to introduce the study of women as a means of providing their story and to eradicate many of the myths and distortions surrounding the lives of women.

While both movements addressed some very real inadequacies, such as paucity faculty, absence and distortion of curriculum content, and programmatic resources in the Academy, neither fully embraced the unique and authentic experiences of women of African descent in America or on the African continent and throughout the African diaspora. Thus, it became imperative to launch major efforts to recognize and include Africana women in the Academy, with a focus on their scholarship—scholarship being at the center of academe.

In 1984, during my first term as president of the National Council for Black Studies, a major item on our agenda as Africana scholars was to include women more fully into the discipline of Africana Studies (Black Studies). In 1983, in preparation for the spring 1986 conference, the first step in implementing that agenda item took place, awarding women scholars with scholarship on theoretical issues. The logic was to ensure that their voices were presented at the level that men's voices had always been heard. Women had always been a part of the discipline, appearing on panels and presenting their empirical data and insights but not as creators of intellectual ideas as compared to the men. One of the women granted a voice in a plenary session at the annual conference of the 1986 National Council for Black Studies was Clenora Hudson-Weems, who set forth the Africana womanist theory, which she followed with numerous articles, such as "Cultural and Agenda Conflicts in Academia: Critical Issues for Africana Women's Studies" (*Western Journal of Black Studies*, Winter 1989); "The Tripartite Plight of Black Women as Reflected in Hurston's *Their Eyes Were Watching God* and Walker's *The Color Purple*" (*Journal of Black Studies*, December 1989); and her culminating volume, *Africana Womanism: Reclaiming Ourselves* (1993).

In my own earlier seminal article in 1992, "Africana Womanist Issues in Black Studies: Towards Integrating Africana Women into Africana Studies," in *The Afro-Centric Scholar*, I outlined my major views on the scarcity of women as highly visible scholars in the discipline and provided recommendations for creating space so as to claim, reclaim, and nurture Africana women scholars, like Hudson-Weems, without whom the discipline could not flourish.

It is refreshing, then, to receive another publication of an exciting new theoretical volume in 2004 from Clenora Hudson-Weems, following *Africana Womanism: Reclaiming Ourselves* in 1993. Now, this same author gives us *Africana Womanist Literary Theory*. Again, she provides "a bold lensing" for literary theory. *Africana Womanist Literary Theory* is an expansion of ideas presented in *Africana Womanism: Reclaiming Ourselves*. It provides an extensive and thorough understanding of the concepts, "nommo/self-naming" and "self-defining." Hudson-Weems believes nothing is more important to a people's existence than naming and defining self. It comes as no surprise, then, that the work takes to task those who have ignored, distorted, or misappropriated all or parts of the theory that she has articulated. Clearly, Hudson-Weems is to be credited with naming, defining, and popularizing an authentic theoretical concept—Africana womanism—for all women of African descent.

This volume, however, does far more than lay claim to a concept. It is lucid in characterizing the Africana womanist as a self-namer and self-definer who is also family centered with a strong grounding in sisterhood and an unyielding belief in positive Africana male-female relationships as foundations for the survival of Africana people and humankind. Further, Hudson-Weem's paradigm frames ideas about Africana women in an authentic way that differs from all other gender-based theories. Moreover, it demonstrates that women in Africana/Black Studies are critical thinkers and have as much to give to the field as its men scholar/theorists. And, by doing this, her model, with its own label, has been set forth to explain a given set of ideas. Both older and younger scholars can emulate such labeling by developing new models, laying claim to them as they position themselves to continue the tradition of Africana women as critical theorists.

In this twenty-first century, no less than in ages past, the need will be great for scholars to provide paradigms and critical theories for understanding society and its various aspects or forms—historical, cultural, literary, social, and the like. Scholars such as Hudson-Weems will be listed among those who have made a difference in the conceptualization, development, and promotion of the discipline of Africana Studies. Just as race has been and continues to be central to Africana Studies and to defining different realities, no less crucial is it to Hudson-Weems' new work, *Africana Womanist Literary Theory*. While voicing the centrality of race, she is also cognizant of the Africana woman's predicament within the dominant culture as being that of a triple victim of racism, classism, and sexism. She nevertheless, prioritizes, maintaining that among these three "isms," the foremost issue for Africana women remains race. In placing Africa at the center of analysis, Hudson-Weems emerges as a truly authentic scholar, one bent on interpreting the black experience from the perspective of authentic black life. In so doing, she sets the reader up for a provocative work— a work that one cannot put down until it is read from cover to cover.

Delores P. Aldridge, Ph.D.
Grace T. Hamilton Chair of Sociology & Black Studies
Emory University

Preface

Every now and then there emerges an idea that is so rich, so ripe and so very revolutionary that the theoretical arena is forever changed. At the same time, it is so simple—deceptively, so immediately identifiable, and so fully verifiable that one has to wonder why no one ever thought of it before. Indeed, you may even (for the briefest of moments) wish *you* had done so. Such is the case of Africana womanism as espoused by Clenora Hudson-Weems, who has shaken the very foundation of Women's Studies in America and abroad with her highly sought after public addresses and numerous publications, including her seminal work, *Africana Womanism: Reclaiming Ourselves*. So, the release of this work, its equally important sequel, is nothing less than a full-fledged event. Why, the chronology of the evolution of the theory of Africana womanism alone makes this book indispensable.

While I was a Ph.D. candidate in Temple University's African American Studies Department, that is, even before hearing about Africana womanism, this writer knew instinctive that something about the notion of feminism did not seem quite right. To say the least, I participated in many a heated debate with a very dear friend, a self-proclaimed feminist, whom I often chide for her "anti-male" stances. So imagine my sense of affirmation upon learning that there actually exists a framework that formalizes my reservations about the polarizing nature of feminism. Immediately I knew that I had to meet this woman-after-my-own-heart. I had to *talk* to her to pick her brain. In addition, my dissertation, "Composite Conjugality Considered: An Afrocentric Study of the Faces of So-called Polygamy in the African Novel" lends itself naturally to Africana womanist literary analysis in some respect. In fact, one chapter focuses heavily on the dynamics of Africana womanist/African feminist theory.

As fate would have it, in the fall of 2000, I learned that Hudson-Weems would be in Philadelphia for an opening plenary presentation at a national/international annual academic conference. With the assistance of my dissertation director, Professor Molefi Kete Asante, I contacted her and was amazed at the relative ease with which I was able to secure a personal interview. The rest, as they say, is history. It was as though I had known this *grande dame* my entire life. After meeting her at the airport, we proceeded to have dinner and to talk for hours. I found myself marveling at her complete lack of self-involvement, especially in view of her secure and historical place in the cannons of Africana Studies. I had only seen this previously in Professors Chinua Achebe and Yoself ben Jochannan, two other legendary, gracious Africana personalities with whom I consulted during my research.

At any rate, I subsequently approached Hudson-Weems, asking her to consider being the external reader on my dissertation committee; she readily agreed. Since then, she has become an invaluable friend and mentor, always encouraging and quietly opening doors, asking nothing in return—except productivity, that is. Which brings me to perhaps the most beautiful and noteworthy thing about Clenora Hudson-Weems: She is not just another theorist whose actions do not reflect her philosophy. She practices what she preaches: that Africana womanism is not just some ideal born in a vacuum, never to be practically applied. Strictly speaking, she is the living embodiment of Africana womanism.

From the beginning, I was struck by her family-centered nature. During our meeting, she was just a bit distracted by her efforts to finalize her daughter Nima's move from Philadelphia to New York. I could feel the love in her voice as she spoke to her and later about her and about her husband, Robert. Afterward, I confided to a good friend and colleague that I had finally found someone who talked about her family more than about herself or her work. It was really a beautiful thing.

Moreover, I can attest to the personal impact that both Africana womanism and Clenora Hudson-Weems have had on my life. Needless to say, my relationship with this courageous daughter of the African diaspora and of the American South was only just beginning on that fateful day in Philadelphia, and I don't use the word "fateful" here lightly. Without question, it was divine guidance that led me to reach out to her, for in so doing, I inadvertently became enveloped in a circle of nurturing sisterhood, the likes of which are rare and life-altering, this at a time when I had begun to lose faith in the notion of genuine sisterhood. Like Toni Morrison in "Cinderella's Stepsisters," I, too, was deeply troubled and traumatized, even by the treachery and chicanery that far too often infuse woman-to-woman interaction, both personally and professionally. In my estimation, this is of particular concern in the Africana community.

Of course, anyone who has been paying even scant attention in recent years knows that, much of the time relations between Africana men and women can be just as dysfunctional. As Hudson-Weems has suggested, many, including myself, are of the opinion that feminism and its attendant "sexual revolution" and "the war of the sexes" are at the root of this critical problem confronting the Africana family. This is not to deny that there are valid issues of sexism that, if left unchecked, threaten the very foundation of the black community, something the Africana womanist and the African feminist can agree upon. So, some may ask, what's the problem? In a word—approach. Therein lies the fundamental difference.

Whereas the feminist tends to focus on gender empowerment to the exclusion of all else, the elevation of the Africana race and community is the center of consciousness for the Africana womanist. A perfect example of this is the case of the late, great Funmilayo Ransome-Kuti (FRK), who, although an avowed feminist, was a nationalist first and foremost and, I would argue, an Africana womanist. Cheryl Johnson-Odim and Nina Emma Mba unconsciously document this well in *For Women and the Nation: Funmilayo Ransome-Kuti of Nigeria* (1997). One of my favorite parts of the biography, which bears early witness to the veracity of Africana womanist analysis, is her poignant comment on the authorship of the Nigerian national anthem, which was composed by "Lady" Flora Lugard, the wife of "Lord" Frederick Lugard, the notorious former colonial governor of Nigeria.

> It is most surprising that it was not possible to find a person within 30,000,000 people cable enough to compose our national anthem. We as women are proud to see that the anthem had been composed by a woman. But we would have wished her to be a Nigerian woman. We hope she will pardon us for this expression. It is only natural that we should feel that. [Johnson-Okim and Mba 99]

Here, the authors attribute FRK's remarks, which clearly reveal a "race-first" philosophy, to her "priority of nationalist feminist allegiance"; however, one could (and should) argue that what it really demonstrates is FRK's Africana womanist belief system, which is on full display in this except from her 1959 speech at the Third Annual

Conference of the Federation of Nigerian Women Societies (FNWS). Moreover, FRK exhibited several other what can only be called classic Africana womanist tendencies. Namely, she was the nurturing mother of four children, including her beloved second son, the late Olufela "Fela" Ransome-Kuti, famed musician and activist, who can only be described as one of Nigeria's national treasures. Mother and son were famously close, and it is believed that it was at his urging that she dropped her given European names, Frances Abigail, and reverted to her African birth name, Funmilayo. She would never legally change her name, but in the 1970s she dropped Ransome and, being the self-namer that she was, selected the middle name Anikulopo, Yoruba for "warrior who carries strong protection" or "hunter who carries death in a pouch" (Johnson-Odim and Mba 1968).

The Ransom-Kuti story segues nicely into my final but I submit, keystone point: Africana womanism is not just a literary concept. Granted, that is the centerpiece of this opus, *Africana Womanist Literary Theory*. Nonetheless, it would be a grievous mistake to conclude that its only application is in the fictional realm, for this would ignore the fullness of the matrix of this groundbreaking doctrine, that encompasses the cultural, the sociological, the political, and, in reality, every area of Africana life.

Yes! That is *it*. When all is said and done, it's about *life*. Case in point, even though Hudson-Weems' insightful theory of Africana womanism would not arrive until 1986, nearly a decade after Funmilayo Ransome-Kuti's death in 1978, her *life* only corroborates Clenora's assertion that she did not *create* the Africana womanist paradigm single-handedly. Rather, after careful examination of the Africana female experience, she simply delineated her clear-cut findings, shaped an authentic paradigm based on those findings, and then proceeded to assign to the total its own name—Africana womanism.

Pamela Yaa Asantewaa Reed, Ph. D.
Chair of Communications & Co-Chair of Humanities/Letters
The College of New Rochelle, School of New Resources

Introduction

Slaves and dogs are named by their masters.
Free men [and women] name themselves.

The above quotation by a 1960s Harlem political activist, Richard B. Moore, is quoted in a seminal article appearing in *African Commentary Magazine* written by the eminent African historian, John Henrik Clarke, in which he expounds upon the cruciality of self-naming and self-defining for Africana people. So is this the case, the *raison d'être*, the very foundation upon which the critical paradigm of Africana Womanism rests. For well over a decade and a half, I have relentlessly insisted that self-naming (*nommo*) and self-defining are at the very core of authentic existence. In my first article on Africana womanism in the late 1980s, I issued the initial call for this important prerequisite for Black women's survival and by extension, Black survival. I called for Africana women worldwide to reclaim, rename, and redefine themselves, using the terminology and concept of Africana womanism, whose term itself evokes a new paradigm of prioritizing the tripartite plight of race, class and gender for all women of African descent, as a new tool for analysis, beginning with the power of the word—*nommo*.

Africana Womanist Literary Theory, the second book on what I consider my life's work, continues and advances my research on the concept of Africana Womanism, which is both family-centered and race-based. Growing out of my first book on the subject, *Africana Womanism: Reclaiming Ourselves* (1993), this book locates and refines the eighteen culturally derived Africana womanist characteristics self-namer, self-definer, family-centered, in concert with male in struggle, genuine in sisterhood, strong, whole, authentic, flexible role player, male compatible, respected, recognized, adaptable, respectful of elders, spiritual, ambitious, mothering and nurturing—originally presented in *Africana Womanism*. More specifically, this new book presents a fully formed theoretical structure of Africana Womanist literary theory, highlighting many of these key descriptors in rendering a truly authentic analysis of Africana women within a cultural and literary context, thereby more accurately reflecting Black life itself. This particular perspective of Africana women is by far more plausible than a superimposed, inapplicable paradigm for Black life and its women. Arguably, feminism, and by extension Black feminism, carries its own baggage that does not work within a Black historical and cultural context. Invariably it either directly or indirectly, overtly or covertly includes anti-male sentiments, and gender exclusivity, or at least the prioritization of gender issues at the risk of downplaying the critical significance of race priority for Africanans. Such baggage cannot be afforded in the Africana community and thus, should not be encouraged, as it would further complicate the crucial concerted struggle of Africana men, women and children for human parity. To be sure, we must insist upon our own historical, political, social, and cultural matrix to interpret and translate our lives in order that our rich African legacy may be handed down for future generations. The following quotation comes from one of my earlier articles on this particular need:

> I cannot stress enough the critical need today for Africana scholars throughout the world to create our own paradigms and theoretical frameworks for assessing our works. We need our own Africana theorists, not scholars who duplicate or use theories created by others in analyzing Africana texts. Indeed, developing paradigms and critical theories, which is our true mission, makes possible for better monitoring interpretations of our works in an effort to keep them both authentic and accurate in order to maintain their originality in meaning and value. The problem, however, is that contrary to white or European theorists, who justifiably approach their literature from the perspective of the centrality of their culture, Eurocentrism, most Africana scholars use theories that are alien and

> have not been passed through our cultural matrix or
> lens. . . . We take the Procrustean approach, via super-
> imposing alien or outside theories and methodolo-
> gies as a primary means of analyzing and interpreting
> our texts from a so-called legitimate, universally the-
> oretical perspective. Be it known that this ruling per-
> spective in reality is none other than just another
> perspective. (Hudson-Weems, . . . "Africana Theory
> and Thought," 79)

Composed of ten chapters, this book establishes the place of Africana womanist theory within both a critical and literary context by consistently applying the theoretical Africana womanists descriptors to various literary texts and moments. Chapter One, *Nommo*/Self-Naming, Self-Defining, and the History of *Africana Womanism*, documents the history, the evolution, and the critical reception of this national and international concept, which reveals that this concept was, in fact, at the center of the seminal debates for nearly two decades surrounding the place of Black women in academia. Despite the fact that many Black feminists have futilely attempted to silence this perspective by refusing to acknowledge its presence or existence, a practice which Jacob H. Carruthers defines in *Intellectual Warfare* as the "time-tested strategy of nonrecognition," Africana womanism has and continues to galvanize Black women activists and academicians. Moreover, notwithstanding the assistance of the Black Feminist Revisionist Project, whose mission continues to be that of reclaiming all Black women activists and writers, including Anna Julia Cooper and Zora Neale Hurston, to name a couple, as feminists based on gender alone, regardless of their focus, Africana womanism successfully continues the race-based legacy of African womanhood. Chapter Two, Cultural and Agenda Conflicts in Academia: Critical Issues for Africana Women's Studies, historicizes the concept of Africana Womanism, which was first announced in print in 1989 in *The Western Journal of Black Studies*, thereby bringing the authentic theory of Africana womanism into the fold of academia, as it traces the debates that accompanied the advent of this framework as a viable and workable meta-theoretical construct. Key pre-Africana womanist orators and activists cited here include Sojourner Truth, Harriet Tubman, and Ida B. Wells. Chapter Three, Africana Womanism:

The Authentic Agenda for Women of African Descent, presents Africana Womanism as a legitimate theoretical methodology for Africana women. This authentication is made possible by bringing into the analysis global Africana women novelists—Nigeria's, Buchi Emecheta and Ghana's Ama Ata Aidoo whose writings on the primacy of race in the world of their works compliment national Africana womanist writers. Chapter Four, Proud Africana Women Activists: A Legacy of Strong, Family-Centered Culture Bearers, documents the activities of the Africana woman as warrior for her people, dating back to Black women in antiquity up to today, including Queen Nzingha and Queen Mother Yaa Asantewa. These powerful Black women are the progenitors of proud Africana women, including nineteenth century abolitionists and literary activists, Maria W. Stewart and Frances Watkins Harper, as well as Paule Marshall, who through her protagonist in *Praisesong for the Widow* (1982) represents the supreme paradigm of the authentic Africana womanist. Chapter Five, Genuine Sisterhood: Or Lack Thereof, expounds upon the critical need and urgency for sisterly relations among Africana women for the betterment of our overall families and communities. In this chapter, Nobel Prize-winning author, Toni Morrison in her novel *Sula,* and in her commencement address, "Cinderella Stepsisters," as well as poet, Mona Lake Jones, and her powerful poem "A Room Full of Sisters," convincingly make a case for the importance of more positive friendships among women. Chapter Six, Africana Male-Female Relationships and Sexism in the Community, makes a strong case for positive interdependency of Africana men and women for human survival in a racially hostile environment in which the entire Black race is victimized. It articulates the penultimate role of the Africana man and woman as harmonious companions both in their personal and political lives, a mission which starts no doubt in the home with a strong, loving family, made possible by a wholesome male-female relationship, an ideal to which international writer, Mariama Bâ, aspires in her defining novel, *So Long A Letter,* as well as Terri McMillan's protagonist, Zora Banks, in *Disappearing Acts.* Chapter Seven, Sister Souljah's *No Disrespect* is an informative chapter on the fictive autobiography of the celebrated hip-hop rapper herself. In this riveting book, the author offers an up-to-date, profound commentary of the totality of Black life, both raw and real. This chapter presents an Africana womanist analysis of the book by focusing on the initial Africana womanist features of the protagonist, who looses herself for a period when she experiences time and again disappointing failed relationships with her male counterparts, but who ultimately comes back to herself in the end, thanks to the genuine sisterhood existing between herself and one of her best friends, Sheri. Chapters Eight and Nine focus on the Nobel Prize-winning author Toni Morrison: Morrison's *Beloved*: All Parts Equal and *Beloved:* From Novel to Movie. The first presents an application of Africana womanism through a critical analysis of Morrison's *Beloved* as an Africana womanist novel in which her protagonists, Sethe and her male counterpart, Paul D., experience shared oppression, an experience that they are able to transcend through their love and vision. The second has an introductory section to a review of the movie, *Beloved*, which continues the dialogue on the importance of race in the validation of Africana womanism, hence, promoting race empowerment, since racism is the salient issue prohibiting ultimate parity for Africana people. The Conclusion, the final chapter, recapitulates the direction of Africana Theory and Thought as it relates to Africana women, with considerations for the implications of an African-centered theoretical methodology for Africana womanist literary criticism.

Africana Womanist Literary Theory, therefore, promises to be an invaluable work, indicated by the on-going current debates with academic discourse on the future position of American/Africana Literature and Criticism, and the growing demand for global and trans-cultural paradigms, particularly within Africana, Post Colonial, and Gender Studies in graduate programs. For example, at the University of Missouri-Columbia, I initiated the Nation's first Africana Concentration for a graduate degree in English, a program which made its debut in 2001, with Africana Theory as its pivotal course. Hence, because of the renewed call for African-centered and derived knowledge bases within literary studies, this seminal work offers an authentic lens through which to conceptualize and analyze Africana women in particular, their lives, their families, and their literary works. To be sure, the important role for the next generation of Africana scholars will be in establishing without compromise the crucial role of the Africana woman, too, who must continue to place the needs of her greater Africana family, who have for centuries suffered racial domination and exploitation, at the top of her list of priorities for ultimate human survival. The challenge for us as Africana scholars, both men and women, then, is to ensure ultimate victory for ourselves, our families, and our future generations as we move forth in the midst of intellectual and physical onslaughts for both our minds and our place in the turbulent world today, including the world of academe. *Africana Womanist Literary Theory* accepts that challenge and advances in a direction best suited for accuracy in authentic literary scholarship, that is creations and interpretations focusing on the totality of Black women's presence within our own rich and unique historical and cultural zones, both inside and outside the Academy.

Clenora Hudson-Weems, Ph.D.
Professor of English
University of Missouri-Columbia

Chapter I

Nommo: Self-Naming, Self-Defining, and the History of *Africana Womanism*

Definitions belonged to the definers—not the defined.
—Toni Morrison, *Beloved*

Africana womanism, emerged from the acknowledgment of a long-standing authentic agenda for that group of women of African descent who needed only to be properly named and officially defined according to their own unique historical and cultural matrix, one that would reflect the co-existence of men and women in a concerted struggle for the survival of their entire family/community. The process by which this phenomenon, a concept I named and defined in the mid-eighties (then called "Black womanism"), took shape, and the open acknowledgment of its pre-existence was articulated in a 1998 publication, several years after my 1992 presentation at the First International Conference on Women of Africa and the African Diaspora at the University of Nigeria-Nsukka:

> For nearly a decade, I have been actively working on naming and defining, via identifying and refining an African-centered paradigm for women of African descent. In observing the traditional role, character, and activity of this collective group, identified by their common African ancestry, I concluded during the early stages of my research that the phenomenon I

1

named and defined as Africana womanism had long
been in existence, dating back to the rich legacy of
African womanhood. Therefore, I did not create the
phenomenon in and of itself, but rather observed
Africana women, documented our reality, and refined
a paradigm relative to who we are, what we do, and
what we believe in as a people. [Hudson-Weems,
"Self-Naming" 449]

The activity surrounding Africana/black womanism itself commenced
in the fall of 1985, when, during my first semester as a Ph.D. student at
the University of Iowa, I challenged Black feminism. At that time I
used the terminology "Black womanism," which later evolved to the
present terminology—Africana womanism. From the research paper I
wrote that semester, entitled "The Tripartite Plight of the Black
Woman—Racism, Classism and Sexism—in *Our Nig, Their Eyes Were
Watching God* and *The Color Purple*," I was motivated to set up a panel
for the 13-16, March 1986 National Council for Black Studies (NCBS)
Annual Conference in Boston. I presented a paper there entitled "Black
Womanism versus Black Feminism—Racism First, Sexism Last: The
Survival of the Black Race," wherein an obvious paradigm is outlined
in the title itself. While many black women at the conference, includ-
ing two established sociologists, Delores Aldridge, then president of the
NCBS, and Vivian Gordon, author of a later publication *Black Women,
Feminism and Black Liberation: Which Way?* (1987), concurred with my
thesis of the prioritization of race, class, and gender respectively, while
others insisted on the simultaneity of these obstacles in the lives of black
women.

For the three years standing, from 1985 to 1988, and even to my
first publication in 1989 on the subject, I relentlessly spoke out on this
crucial subject at national conferences, most notably at a panel entitled
"The Tripartite Plight of Black Women" for the 24-28, June 1987
National Women's Studies Association Convention in Atlanta, Georgia.
That fall, the challenge presented to my work on black women con-
tinued and was taken up on an Iowa City local television program,
"The Silver Tongue," where I debated a senior doctoral student, who
would complete her studies there in 1989, approximately a year after
I did. Later that semester, I continued to challenge Black feminism in

a paper presented at a 1987 University of Iowa Black Survival Conference: "Black Womanism versus Black Feminism: A Critical Issue for Human Survival." The seed for two subsequent presentations came from this work, with some revisions—work that was well received at the 7-9, April 1988 National Council for Black Studies and later at the 28-30, April 1988 African Heritage Studies Association Annual Conferences. In fact, some of my colleagues acknowledged that feminism/black feminism, for some reason or another, did not quite work for them, and they expressed their gratitude for this new distinction.

The following year, the fruition of this long continuous work culminated in two publications: One was "Cultural and Agenda Conflicts in Academia: Critical Issues for Africana Women's Studies" which was released in the 1989 Winter issue of *The Western Journal of Black Studies*. The other was "The Tripartite Plight of African-American Women as Reflected in the Novels of Hurston and Walker" which was released in the December 1989 issue of *The Journal of Black Studies*. A call for new terminology for articulating the historical and cultural reality of women of African descent was issued forth in the first article:

> Africana women might begin by naming and defining their unique movement "Africana Womanism." The concept of Womanism can be traced back to Sojourner's [1852] speech that began to develop and highlight Africana women's unique experience into a paradigm for Africana women. [Hudson-Weems, "Cultural and Agenda Conflicts" 187]

This new terminology, coupled with a new paradigm, expressed discontent with other female-based constructs (e.g.: feminism, black feminism, and womanism) that had not clearly expressed an agenda for Africana women relative to the prioritizing of their triple plight. To be sure, this sense of prioritizing is clearly delineated in Sojourner Truth's self actualization oration "And Ain't I a Woman," where she was obligated to address the race factor first, then the class factor, before she could even begin to entertain the absurd notion of female subjugation, the gender factor.

Four years later, in 1993, the publication of the book on this topic, *Africana Womanism: Reclaiming Ourselves,* was released, despite the fact

3

that several publishers initially expressed hesitancy in publishing the manuscript. Their reluctance was in no small part due to the controversial issues surrounding black women's rejection of "mainstream" feminist ideology, that is, its caustic beginnings and its inapplicability for women of African descent. Significantly, *Africana Womanism* was at the center of existing debates and at the forefront of a new, even bolder controversy in its radical pronouncement of the abandonment of feminist terminology in labeling black women. Describing my work in the biographical head-notes preceding my contributed article to their text, the editors of *Call and Response: The Riverside Anthology of the African American Literary Tradition* asserted the following:

> Taking a strong position that black women should not pattern their liberation after Eurocentric feminism but after the historic and triumphant women of African descent, Hudson Weems has launched a new critical discourse in the Black Women's Literary Movement. [Hill 1811]

At the same time, those black women (black feminists) who continued to use the term feminism as a theoretical construct for their analysis received unnumbered support for their research. Aligning themselves with the acceptable framework of feminism was unquestionably one of the most reliably strategic means of becoming initiated into that established community, which rendered many perks, such as visibility, prodigious employment possibilities, and publications. Clearly, such a *reward system* has been influential in black feminists and black feminist critics' allegiance to and identification with dominant feminist ideologies. Moreover, it is my conjecture that many may very well have viewed their acceptance of Africana womanism not only as risking their professional security, but as invalidating their years of research from the Black feminist perspective. This, indeed, is unfortunate, for instead they should have viewed "it as a natural evolutionary process of ideological growth and development" for the black women's movement from black feminism to Africana womanism (Hudson-Weems, "... Entering the New Millennium" 36). In the final analysis, then, in an attempt to reshape the feminist/black feminist agenda to suit their needs by ignoring an existing practical, theoretical, and more compatible construct, these prominent black feminists, having been "appropriated and reshaped into a revised form of black feminism," often duplicate much of the work that has already been done in Africana womanism, distinguishable only, for the most part, by misnaming (Hudson-Weems, "Africana Womanism: An Overview" 206).

Exemplifying this practice is black feminist Evelyn Brooks Higginbotham in "African-American Women's History and the Metalanguage of Race," published in 1992, approximately six years after the inception of many powerful debates and publications delineating the importance of self-naming and self-defining for black women, which encompasses formulating one's own name, agenda, and priorities as highlighted in black womanism/Africana womanism. To be sure, Higgenbotham was well aware of the fact that race had not been properly factored into the burgeoning field of Women's Studies, and thus, she called for "Feminist scholars, especially those of African-American women's history, [to] accept the challenge to bring race more prominently into their analysis of power" (Higginbotham 3), a call issued several years earlier in the announcement of Africana womanism. Black feminist bell hooks, who unrealistically urged black women to move from the peripheral to the center of the feminist movement, which was founded by white women and justifiably tailored to their particular needs, later incorporated many of the descriptors outlines in *Africana Womanism* in one of her mid-nineties publications. Moreover, Patricia Hill Collins, in a 1995 article, "What's in a Name? Womanism, Black Feminism, and Beyond," inaccurately asserts that "No term currently exists that adequately represents the substance of what diverse groups of black women alternately call womanism and black feminism" (Collins 17). The truth of the matter is that the so-called non-existent term to which Collins refers had already been articulated years before in *Africana Womanism*, which was, at the time of her article, in its third revised edition. As the term Africana womanism had been in existence since the mid-eighties, it is clear that, along with the terminology, a well-defined paradigm was also established. Even Alice Walker's "womanism" pronouncments—literally a page and one-half—does little more than present a brief commentary on the shade differentiation between what Collins notes as "alternately call[ed] womanism and black feminism"—purple vs. lavender. (See Walker's introduction to her collection of essays entitled *In Search of Our Mother's*

Gardens.) Restating in her own words what Africana womanism had pronounced a decade earlier, but without any reference to *Africana Womanism* itself, Collins contends:

> Several difficulties accompany[ing] the use of the term "black feminism" ... involves the problem of balancing the genuine concerns of black women against continual pressures to absorb and recast such interests within white feminist frameworks... the emphasis on [of white feminist] themes such as personal identity, understanding "difference" ... and the simplistic model of the political ... "personal is political," that currently permeate North American white women's feminism in the academy can work to sap black feminism of its critical edge. [15]

More important than the way the Academy, in collusion with feminism, has effectively diluted the "critical [black feminist] edge" is the tacit consent that black feminism has given both to the Academy and white feminism through its short-sighted forfeiture of the highly political edge that Africana womanism offers. Even as black feminism attempts to correct its myopic vision through its incorporation of the substance of Africana womanism, it fails to admit (while it omits) Africana womanism's essential and underlying foundation—*nommo,* its name.

Collins' own shift to what she incorrectly claims to be a more culturally/globally centered approach to theorizing black women's resistance to all oppression is even more pronounced in her tenth and most recent edition of *Black Feminist Thought* (2000). Here she vividly points to the confusion and dysfunctionality that the term Black feminism engenders: "whereas this edition remains centered on U.S. black women, it raises questions concerning African American women's positionality within a global black feminism" (xii). Obviously, this type of confusion and these types of questions with regard to Africana women within any type of feminism is directly and clearly addressed within the authentic agenda put forth by Africana womanism. Conversely, scholarship like that expressed in Collins' black feminism finds itself in a socio linguistic and cultural maze. Sadly, Collins demonstrates, through her own language, confusion about what aspects of black feminism she sees as part of a global address/appendage—Africana womanism's prioritizing race, class, and gender-based paradigm or white feminism's gender-based system. Collins' misnaming of black women's resistance and thought through supposed "renaming" or appropriation of a "black" additive to an already baggage-laden feminist center does much to belie her claims to "global black feminism" and most certainly supports Africana womanism's long-standing argument concerning the inherent and fundamental contradiction in the concept of black feminism itself. Collins unwittingly turns a light of truth on her own flawed system of naming as she addresses the problem of terminology with regard to paradigms like Afrocentricity. She glaringly and perhaps unconsciously supports Africana womanism's thesis about the importance of naming and the incongruent relationship between the theory and practice of black feminism and the Africana women it claims to represent. Thus, Collins' contends that "When the same language continues to be used, whereas the meaning attached to it changes . . . the term becomes too value laden to be useful" (Collins xi). Her assertion here, which she later contradicts, clearly echoes and appropriates the underlying premise for Africana womanism without so much as citing the source—as scholars must ethically do. For example, in "Cultural and Agenda Conflicts in Academia: Critical Issues for Africana Women's Studies," I insisted that "When the Black feminist buys the White terminology, she also buys its agenda" (Hudson'Weems, "Cultural" 188). Collins contradicts her notion of a non-existing alternative terminology for black women in her earlier publication, "What's in a Name?," yet later acknowledges its existence in *Black Feminist Thought*, tenth edition, in which she lists alternative terminologies:

> Rather than developing definitions and arguing over
> naming practices—for example, whether this thought
> should be called Black feminism, womanism, Afrocentric
> feminism, Africana womanism, and the like—a more
> useful approach lies in revisiting the reasons why black
> feminist thought exists at all. [Collins 22]

Clearly, from this quotation, we see that she has missed the point. Obviously she does not comprehend the concept of *nommo*, or she would not have ended by proposing such a question in the first place.

More relevant is the question of why Collins retains the term, "feminist" and refuses a more authentic one? This is the dilemma within which black feminism, through its dysfunctional association with gender and illogical disassociation from race, finds itself. Pointing to the relationship between terminology, Africana womanism, and its potential for effecting political change, Afrocentric scholar Ama Mazama highlights Hudson-Weems' Africana womanism in rendering particularly useful contributions to the Afrocentric discourse on African women and men. "Clenora Hudson-Weems coined the term *Africana Womanism* in 1987 out of the realization of the total inadequacy of feminism and like theories (e.g., Black feminism, African womanism, or womanism) to grasp the reality of African women, let alone give us the means to change that reality" [Mazama 400].

Notwithstanding the failure of black feminists to utilize Africana womanism as a tool for analyzing Africana women's lives, and the way this original paradigm has affected our perception and fostered a deeper understanding of our agenda in the past twelve to fifteen years is evident. But the voice of Africana womanism will not and cannot be silenced, and like the true Africana womanist, who has never really needed to "break silence" or to "find voice," the expressed sentiments of many feminists, I have continued—through my ever-evolving critical paradigm—to uphold the Africana womanist agenda and priorities within Africana historical and cultural contexts. Such contexts are reflected in our on going struggle for the human rights of our entire family—men, women, and children.

Using Africana womanism as a spring board, Valethia Watkins, in "Womanism and Black Feminism: Issues in the Manipulation of African Historiography," interrogates Nancie Caraway's critique of the failure of white feminists to document black women's role in the feminist movement. While Caraway's critique appears a sincere gesture to "correct" the past regarding its omission of black women from the feminist arena, the Black Feminist Revisionist Project, a response to Caraway's work, was flawed at its inception for various reasons. To begin with, the very intent and design of the project to reclaim *all* black women as feminists, particularly activists in our on-going liberation struggle—e.g.: Sojourner Truth, Harriet Tubman, Anna Julia Cooper, Ida B. Wells, Rosa Parks—presupposes the primacy of a white history of resistance. Thus, the Black Revisionist Project problematically locates black activism, dating back in antiquity, outside of its historical reality. In other words, naming black women activists after white women, black feminists, is in essence "duplicating a duplicate," since in reality, feminists often modeled their strategies after black activist models, such as antislavery abolitionism, the civil rights movements, and other political frameworks for survival that are found in black history and black communities (Hudson-Weems, *Africana Womanism* 22). In fact, they go so far as to claim any and all activities and perspectives related to (black) women as black feminist.

One blatant example of this is in placing Toni Morrison's 1971 *New York Times Magazine* article "What the Black Woman Thinks about Women's Lib" in a 2000 feminist publication entitled *Radical Feminism*, edited by Barbara A. Crow, which, by its very inclusion in this feminist text of such a title, presumes or more significantly suggests that the article belongs to a feminist arena. In that article, Morrison is clearly not espousing a feminist agenda for female empowerment; rather she asserts, "the early image of Women's Lib was of an elitist organization made up of upper-middle class women with the concerns of class and not paying much attention to the problems of most black women" (Morrison, quoted in *Radical Feminism*, 455). Moreover, in Wendy Harding and Jacky Martin's *A World of Difference: An Intercultural Study of Toni Morrison's Novels*, which was published in 1994, quoted Morrison as saying that she "feels too much emphasis is placed on gender politics," and hence her emphasis on the cruelties and horrific after effects of slavery are justified (Harding 61). If anything, her focus here is on race—i.e., on the exclusion of black women's concerns. And this is only two examples of unconscionable acts in the academy.

Tragically, dating back to the inception of the Black Feminist Revisionist Project, black women scholars, according to this project's documentation, stood "silent" on mislabeling black women activists, thinkers, etc. as black feminists. Critiquing this practice, Watkins contends:

> Despite the sheer magnitude and scope of the Black Feminist Revisionist Project, it has gone virtually unchallenged, and it has been met with silence, by and large, by the community of African-centered scholars. One notable exception to our complicity

with this project, through our silence, has been a critical commentary written by Clenora Hudson-Weems
. . . [who] contends that this revisionist process of
inappropriately labeling African women is both arbi-
trary and capricious. Similarly, she argues that a feminist procrustean agenda de-emphasizes and recasts
the primary concern of African women of the nineteenth and early twentieth century. According to
Hudson-Weems, the primary concern of the women
and men of this era was the life-threatening plight of
African people, male and female. Black feminist revi-
sionism changes this focus into a narrow feminist
concern, which prioritizes the plight of women as
delinked and somehow different from the condition
of the men in their community. [258]

Of course, refusal to surrender the authentic agenda for Africana
women, notwithstanding the many personal and professional sacrifices, has paved the way for contemporary black women to follow,
even though many, some of them are cited above, have failed to
acknowledge Africana womanism as a legitimate paradigm and model.
They have too often camouflaged their so called "new black feminism," as proposed by Hortense Spillers, wherein they can more equally
deal with gender and race issues, suggesting that an adequate model of
resistance against female oppression for black women in a racist society does not already exist within Africana cultures and society. With their
revised theory, they position themselves straddling the fence and thus,
remain ideologically acceptable by the dominant culture.

It should be here noted here that in the wake of more recognition
of the cultural diversity that exists within the general population and
by extension its concomitant global perspectives on gender, the dominance of mainstream gender perspectives is waning and Africana
womanism, at the center of the debate for well over a decade and a
half, is at the forefront of this transcultural revisitation of a woman's
place in society. In addition to an interview that Kay Bonetti conducted in 1995 for *The American Audio Prose Library, Inc.* on *Africana
Womanism*, many scholars have asked me for chapters, articles, or reprints
of my work that deal with Africana womanism for their publications.

Thus, my work has been included in such publications as *Call and Response: The Riverside Anthology of the African American Literary Tradition* (1997); *A Historiographical and Bibliographical Guide to the African American Experience* (2000); *Out of the Revolution: The Development of Africana Studies* (2000); *Sisterhood, Feminisms and Power* (1998); and *State of the Race, Creating Our 21st Century* (2004). In my edited book entitled *Contemporary Africana Theory and Thought* (2004), there is an entire section devoted to scholarship on the application of Africana womanism. Additionally, I was contributing editor for a special issue on *Africana womanism* for the 2002 Spring Issue of *The Western Journal of Black Studies*, which includes several articles by Africana womanist scholars at various universities in various disciplines. Thus, Africana womanism is indisputably creating a new wave for black women and the black women's movement in particular on all fronts.

Be that as it may, many were impressed with this new paradigm from the very beginning, and I received numerous invitations to speak at institutions across the nation, including an invitation from Winston-Salem State University's 1988 Black History Month Program, where I had the occasion to meet and converse with renowned scholar, the late Dr. C. Eric Lincoln, Professor Emeritus of Duke University, who endorsed *Africana Womanism: Reclaiming Ourselves*.

> Hudson-Weems's *Africana Womanism* sent unaccustomed shock waves through the domain of popular thinking about feminism, and established her as a careful, independent thinker, unafraid to unsettle settled opinion. [Lincoln quoted in *Africana Womanism*]

Demands for colloquy on this controversial topic grew, complimented by invited speaking engagements—sometimes as many as fifteen a year on this subject alone—at such national/international colleges and universities as the University of Nigeria-Nsukka, University of Utah, Bryn Mawr College, Mary Washington University, Cornell University, Texas Southern University, Illinois Wesleyan University, University of Rhode Island, Central State University, University of Michigan-Flint, University of Illinois-Springfield, LeMoyne-Owen College, Northern Illinois University, Kean University, Drew University, California State University-Long Beach, Virginia Commonwealth

University, Wayne State University, Stillman College, Southern Utah State University, Kentucky State University, University of Wisconsin-Milwaukee, Temple University, University of the West Indies-Barbados, Miami University, Oxford at Hamilton, Rust College, and the University of Gwelph (Canada). In addition to numerous invitations as guest speaker at institutions of higher learning, I have also been the keynote, plenary, round-table, banquet and luncheon speaker at national/international conventions, among them the National Council for Black Studies Annual Conference, the African Heritage Studies Association Annual Conference, the Annual Meeting of The Association for the Study of African American Life and History, College Language Association Annual Conference, the International Conference on Women of Africa and the African Diaspora, Chicago State University's Black Writers' Annual Conference, the Annual Third World Conference, the National Conference on Civil/Human Rights of Africananas, the Annual Diop International Conference, and the U.S. Army Ft. Leonard Wood Black History Month Luncheon (keynote address). Finally, faculty in several institutions of higher learning in far away places like New Zeland, England, South Africa, Germany, Nigeria, Brazil, Japan, the Caribbean Islands, utilize *Africana Womanism*. National universities also utilize it, among them California State University-Long Beach, University of North Texas, Florida A & M University, Western Michigan University, Indiana State University, Northern Illinois University, San Francisco State University, Temple University, the University of Arizona, the University of Michigan-Flint, the University of Missouri-Columbia, and the University of Utah to name a few.

Having presented the history of the emergence, evolution, and subsequent dominance of Africana womanism, I will now turn to a brief history of the critical acceptance of Africana womanism within cultural and literary studies, focusing on the relationship of these endorsements to the specific agenda. The Editors of *Call and Response: The Riverside Anthology of the African American Literary Tradition* credited me as the "first African American woman intellectual to formulate a position on Africana womanism [in her] groundbreaking study *Africana Womanism: Reclaiming Ourselves*" (Hill 1811).

In the foreword to *Africana Womanism*, the late 'Zula Sofola, the internationally renown scholar revered as Nigeria's first female playwright, describes the work as "not simply a scholarly work, one of those in the mainstream, but our own. It is a new trail blazed with incontrovertible revelations on the African heritage and gender question. Hudson-Weems bravely takes the bull by the horns, confronts the Eurocentric avalanche of works on questions of gender, and puts forward the Afrocentric point of view." [Quoted in *Africana Womanism* xvii]

Daphne Ntiri-Queman, the Sierra Leonean scholar recognized as an expert on women's issues, spent years as a delegate to the United Nations and consultant to Senegal, Kismayo, and Somalia under the auspices of UNESCO, and in her Introduction to *Africana Womanism* she insists:

> This landmark pioneering treatise of Africana woman's realities cannot be ignored. . . . It will unlock closed doors and usher in a spirit of renewed plentitude. *Africana Womanism* is reminiscent of a comparable avant garde movement of the 1930s by diasporan [sic] Black scholars Leopold Sedar Senghor, Leon Damas, and Aime Cesaire, who struggled to seek reassurance of their blackness. [Quoted in *Africana Womanism* 10-11]

In "The WAAD Conference and Beyond: A Look at Africana Womanism," in *Sisterhood, Feminisms and Power: From Africa to the Diaspora*, Ntiri Queman contends that "Its [Africana womanism's] purpose is multifunctional as it serves as the conceptual tool which harnesses the transformative energies and strategies embedded in Africana women's rise from oppression" (Ntiri 462). Later in "Africana Womanism: Coming of Age" in [*Contemporary Africana Theory and Thought*], she concludes:

> Just as there are compelling reasons to reclaim the power to ascribe names to African people (e.g., colored, Negro, African, African-American) in the United States (to reaffirm their race and establish stronger African affinity), so are there reasons to advocate an

Africana womanist theory that is properly labeled, more attuned, and appropriate to the needs of the Africana woman.

Delores Aldridge, holder of an Endowed Chair in Sociology and Africana American Studies at Emory University, endorsed the book in 1993 as "unquestionably a pioneering effort whose time has come." Her edited book, *Out of the Revolution: The Development of Africana Studies*, in which I have contributed a chapter, Her article, "Towards Integrating Africana Women into Africana Studies," presents her juxtaposition of Black women's activities and Africana Studies with Women's Studies. Here she discusses the history of the caustic beginnings of feminism as presented in *Africana Womanism*, which cites Carrie Capman Catt's contention that white men must recognize "the usefulness of woman suffrage as a counterbalance to the foreign vote, and as a means of legally preserving white supremacy in the South" (quoted in Hudson-Weems, *Africana Womanism*, 21). Aldridge concludes, "it is from this perspective of Africana womanism that this discourse [on integrating Africana women in Africana Studies] is developed" (Aldridge 193). She also refers to my thesis on Africana womanism as a "revolutionary work [that] has no parallel as a new way of understanding Africana women" (196). Finally, in her forthcoming article "Black Male-Female Relationships: An African Centered Lens Model" in the book *Contemporary Africana Theory and Thought*, she adds me to her "chorus of voices [that] have criticize [d] feminism" (LaRue, 1970, Duberman, 1975, Gordon, 1987, [and] Hudson-Weems, 1989 and 1993).

Talmadge Anderson Professor Emeritus at Washington State University, and Founding Editor for *The Western Journal of Black Studies*, concludes in his book endorsement that the "work captures the essence of the true meaning of Black womanhood and resolves the classical debate relative to the prioritizing of race, class and sex in American society." Similarly, Robert Harris, vice provost and former chair of the Africana Studies and Research Center at Cornell University, asserts the following:

In the triple marginality of Black women, race rises above class and gender in this remarkable book. With

14

it, a reunion, a much needed healing, a human philosophy emerges for men and women of African
ancestry and ultimately for all caring men and women.
[Quoted in *Africana Womanism*]

The late Maria Mootry, respected literary critic, original Black Bio-ethi-
cist, and author of the seminal work in this area, "Confronting
Racialized Bioethics: New Contract on Black America" (*Western Journal
of Black Studies* 2000), taken from her unpublished manuscript *Brain
Games: Race, Bioethics and the Seduction of the American Mind*, stated the
following in her review of *Africana Womanism*:

> Now comes a voice, cool and clear, rising above the
> chorus, offering not only lucid insights into the status
> of Africana women and their literature, but a blue-
> print to help us find a way out of confusion and
> despair. In *Africana Womanism: Reclaiming Ourselves*, in
> its second revised edition after only seven months,
> Clenora Hudson-Weems examines the perceptions
> women in the African diaspora have of their histor-
> ical and contemporary roles. She treads fearlessly
> through the maze of tension between mainstream
> feminism, Black feminism, African feminism, and
> Africana Womanism. The result, in the words of
> Professor Charles Hamilton, is "an intellectual tri-
> umph." [244]

Daisy Lafond, former editor of *Voice: The Caribbean International
Magazine*, writes the following in *Class Magazine*:

> Molefe Kete Asante gave us Afrocentricity, to help us
> relocate ourselves from the margins of European expe-
> riences to the centrality of our own. Now, Clenora
> Hudson-Weems, in her second book *Africana
> Womanism: Reclaiming Ourselves*, is helping black women
> relocate themselves from the margins of white feminism
> to the centrality of their own experiences. [Lafond 57]

15

Finally, April Langley proclaims, in "Lucy Terry Prince: The Cultural and Literary Legacy of Africana Womanism," in *The Western Journal of Black Studies*, that

> It is Africana Womanism as originated, developed, and outlined by Hudson-Weems that enables a reading which restores and revises the African origins of the earlier African American writing. . . . the import of this critical paradigm for the earliest Africana writers is essential for recuperating what is "African" in early African American literature. [Langley 158]

Other scholars who view Africana womanism as a viable concept include P. Jane Splawn ("Recent Developments in Black Feminist Literary Scholarship: A Selective Annotated Bibliography?" in *Modern Fiction Studies*, 1993; Philip L. Kilbride ("Africana Womanism" in *Plural Marriages for Our Times: A Reinvented Option?*, 1994); Mary Ebun Modupe Kolawole (*Womanism and African Consciousness*, 1997); Tolagbe Ogunleye, aka: Dr. Martin Ainsi ("African Women and the Grassroots: The Silent Partners of the Women's Movement" in *Sisterhood, Feminisms, and Power: From Africa to the Diaspora*, 1998); Robson Delany, (Ninteenth-Century Africana Womanist: Reflections on His Avant-Garde Politics Concerning Gender, Colorism, and Nation Building" in *The Journal of Black Studies*, 1998); Olabisi Regina Jennings ["Why I Joined the Black Panther Party: An Africana Womanist Reflection" in *The Black Panther Party Reconsidered*, 1998, "Africana Womanism in the Black Panther Party: A Person Story" in *The Western Journal of Black Studies*, 2002 and "Africana Womanist Interpretation of Gwendolyn Brooks' in *Maud Martha*, 2002]; (First International Conference on Women in Africa and the African Diaspora: A View from the USA in *Sisterhood*, 1998); Janette Y. Taylor ("Womanism: A Methodologic Framework for African American Women" in *Advances in Nursing Science*, 1998); P. S. Brush ("The Influence of Social-Movements on Articulations of Race and Gender in Black Women's Autobiography" in *Gender and Society*, 1999); Yolanda Hood ("Africana Womanism and Black Feminism: Re-reading African Women's Quilting Traditions," AFS Annual Meeting, 1999); Laverne Gyant ("The Missing Link: Women in Black/Africana Studies" in *Out of the Revolution: The Development of Africana Studies*,

2000); Carolyn Kumah ("African Women and Literature" in *West Africa Review*, 2000); Deborah Plant ("African Gender Trouble and Africana Womanism: An Interview with Chikwenye Ogunyemi and Wanjira Muthoni" in *Signs*, 2000); JoAnne Banks Wallace ("Womanist Ways of Knowing: Theoretical Considerations for Research with African American Woman" in *Advances in Nursing Science*, 2000); Madhu Kishwar ("Feminism, Rebellious Women and Cultural Boundaries: Re-reading Flora Nwapa and Her Compatriots," 2001); Ama Mazama ("The Afrocentric Paradigm: Contours and Definitions" in *The Journal of Black Studies*, 2001); Adele Newson-Horst ("Gloria Naylor's *Mama Day*: An Africana Womanist Reading" in *Contemporary Africana Theory and Thought*, 2004); ("Maud Martha Brown: A Study in Emergence" in *Maud Martha: A Critical Collection*, 2002); Pamela Yaa Assantewaa Reed ("*Africana Womanism* and *African Feminism*: A Dialectic" in *The Western Journal of Black Studies*, 2001); Anne Steiner ("Frances Watkins Harper: Eminent Pre-Africana Womanist" in *Contemporary Africana Theory and Thought*, 2004); Betty Taylor Thompson [("Common Bonds from the U.S. to Africa and Beyond: Africana Womanist Literary Analysis" in *The Western Journal of Black Studies*, 2001) and (*Contemporary Africana Theory and Thought*, 2004)]; Antonio Tillis (*Hispanic Journal*, "Nancy Morejon's Mujer Negra: An Africana Womanist Reading" in 2001), Barbara Wheeler ("Africana Womanism: An African Legacy— It Ain't Easy Being a Queen" in *Contemporary Africana Theory and Thought*, 2002). Theoretical constructs that have been influenced by Africana womanism include Kawaida womanism, emerging from Maulana Karenga's Kawieda, and Afrocentric womanism, coming out of the school of Afrocentricity as popularized by Molefe Asante.

Even those who have either consciously or unconsciously appropriated Africana womanism demonstrate the overarching presence and validity of this concept. Notably, we have among many Tuzyline Jita Allan (*Womanist and Feminist Aesthetics*); Doris M. Boutain ("Critical Nursing Scholarship: Exploring Critical Social Theory with African American Studies" in *Advances in Nursing Science*, 1999); Michelle Collison ("Race Women Stepping Forward" in *Black Issues in Higher Education* 1999); Nah Dove ("African Womanism: An Afrocentric Theory" in *Sage*, 1998); Lynnett Harvey (*Why Black Women Reject Feminism: Racism in the Feminist Movement*, 1997); Anthonia Kalu ("Women in African Literature," *African Transitions* 2000); and Gail M.

Presby ("Culture, Multiculturalism, and Intercultural Philosophy" in *Forum for Intellectual Philosophizing,* 2000).

Considering the history, the acceptance, and the pronounced demand for its dynamic critical framework, I have been challenged to re-articulate and to further develop the critical principles of Africana womanism. Since Africana people have long been denied not only the authority of naming self, but, moreover, of defining self (as inferred by the narrator of Nobel prize-winning author, Toni Morrison's *Beloved*—"Definitions belonged to the definers—not the defined") it is now of utmost importance that we take control over both these determining interconnected factors in our lives if we hope to avoid degradation, isolation, and annihilation in a world of greed, violence and pandemonium (190). Self-namer and self-definer, two of the eighteen characteristics of the Africana woman, are seminal descriptors that delineate the first step in establishing an authentic paradigm relative to the true level of struggle for women of African descent, as this gets to the very crux of the matter and the history of Africana womanism. From the authentic act of self-naming and self-defining, this critical paradigm emerged. At its very core/center lies *nommo,* an African term that cultural theorist, Molefi Kete Asante, calls "the generative and productive power of the spoken word" (Asante 17). It is a powerful and useful concept holding that the proper naming of a thing will in turn give it essence. Particularizing and advancing the concept, Harrison contends that "Nommo, in the power of the word . . . activates all forces from their frozen state in a manner that establishes concreteness of experience . . . be they glad or sad, work or play, pleasure or pain, in a way that preserves [one's] humanity" (Harrison xx). In African cosmology, the word *nommo,* then, evokes material manifestation. Thus, as Barbara Christian summarizes, "It is through nommo, the correct naming of a thing, that it comes into existence" (157-158), a profound statement to which she herself failed to adhere to calling herself a black feminist. While initiating a call for proper naming, I also insisted on our own agenda and our particular priorities of race, class, and gender contrary to the feminists' female-centered agenda with female empowerment as their number one priority. The other descriptors outlined in *Africana Womanism* are family-centered in concert with the men in the liberation struggle, strong, genuine in sisterhood, whole, authentic, respected, recognized, male compatible, flexible role player, adaptable, respectful of elders, spiritual, ambitious, mothering, and nurturing.

The long-standing focus on the woman and her role in the greater society continues to be at the center of controversy today. For over a century and a half, dating back to pre-Civil War/Emancipation Proclamation, women have been engaged in shaping their role within the context of a particular social reality, one in which white males predominate within a racist patriarchal system. Although racism is clearly a seminal component of the overall system of oppression, white women in general, and the feminist movement in particular, have both been driven almost exclusively by issues related solely to gender oppression. However, the vast majority of black women have necessarily focused their energies on combating racism first before addressing the gender question. As a consequence, it is clear that the two groups ultimately have disparate goals for meeting their specific needs. In short, for black women, who are family-centered, it is race empowerment; for white women, who are female-centered, it is female empowerment. Because of this difference in agendas, distinct naming, then, is critical.

Noted black psychologist Julia Hare makes a profound comment on the reality of the difference in the politics of black life and that of white life, particularly in terms of the difference in certain meanings and ideals relative to the two parallel groups.

> Women who are calling themselves black feminists
> need another word that describes what their con-
> cerns are. Black feminism in not a word that describes
> the plight of black women. In fact, ... black feminists
> have not even come together and come to a true core
> definition of what black feminism is. The white race
> has a woman problem because the women were
> oppressed. Black people have a man and woman prob-
> lem because Black men are as oppressed as their
> women. [Quoted in Phillip, 15]

Hare's 1993 call for another name for the black woman's movement, because of the problematic dynamics of the terminology black feminism, offers insights into the significance of self-naming, and by extension self-definition, for the integrity and survival of Africana people. While her call indicates that she was unaware of the existence of the term Africana womanism as a paradigm for all women of African descent, dating back to the eighties, her seminal statement, nonetheless, echoes the underlying concept of Africana womanism in the ongoing undercurrent debate both within and beyond the Academy surrounding the politics of black and white life. What is particularly disturbing here is the dominant culture's failure to acknowledge proper names, identifications, and systems even when they do exist, as is the case of Africana womanism. Rather, the dominant culture too often promotes distortions of black life and models, the one constancy in an ever-changing climate of dissension and confusion revolving around the lives and destinies of black women and their families. Commanding different terminologies to reflect different meanings, this proper self-naming and self-defining, as a means of establishing clarity, will at the same time offer the first steps towards correcting confusion and misconception regarding one's true identity and the true level of one's struggle in terms of agenda. Hare's statement, then, reflects the nuances of the relativity of a particular terminology and concept—feminism—as issued forth by whites, and its inapplicability to black women as well as their male counterparts who are trapped first and foremost by the race factor rather than by the gender factor so prevalently addressed today. Hence, it is the crucial need for self-naming and self-defining, an interconnecting phenomenon, that becomes penultimate as we come to understand truly that *giving name to* a particular thing simultaneously gives it meaning.

Because of the critical race factor for blacks, another scholar, Audrey Thomas McCluskey, insists that "Black women must adopt a culturally specific term to describe their racialized experience," as she is astutely cognizant of that reality for black women, whether or not black women on the whole pursue this issue to the point of independently naming themselves. McCluskey contends, "the debate over names reflects deeper issues of the right to self-validation and to claim intellectual traditions of their own" (McCluskey 2). Another scholar, Linda Anderson Smith, also writes about the importance of naming. In her article, "Unique Names and Naming Practices among African American Families," she asserts:

> Names are universally recognized as having power—
> as evoking images or signifying membership in a par-
> ticular collective. Names are of great significance to

African Americans, who, because of the history of slavery, have had to fight for the right to choose their names." [Smith 290]

Ben L. Martin, too, notes the importance of naming in "From Negro to Black to African American: The Power of Names and Naming," where he states that "names can be more than tags; they can convey powerful imagery. So naming—proposing, imposing, and accepting names—can be a political exercise" (Martin 83).

While this process seems to be a natural course of action, society, on the contrary, has not taken this route. Rather, it has ignored the true operational existence of this long-standing phenomenon and has elected to name and define Africana women outside of their cultural and historical context via the superimposition of an alien construct—Eurocentrism/feminism. In essence, the dominant culture has held the position of identifying who we are and how we fit into the scheme of things with little regard for what we ourselves perceive as our authentic reality and identity. Instead of respecting our lives as representative of self-authentication, the dominant culture obtrudes itself upon Africana people. Pointing to Africana womanism as a successful strategy and corrective for this obtrusion, Mazama asserts that "the term Africana womanism itself is the first step toward defining ourselves and setting goals that are consistent with our culture and history. In other words, it is the first step toward existing on our own terms" (Mazama 400-401). It must be noted here that "it is true that if you do not name and define yourself, some else surely will" (Hudson-Weems, "Africana Womanism and the Critical Need" 83). And they usually do so miserably. Thus, in the midst of this legacy of continued European domination through improper identification, Africana people must actively reclaim their identity, beginning with self-naming and self-defining. To be sure, without reinventing pre-existing wheels, we could then move more expediently towards resolving the problems of human survival through family cohesiveness, which Africana womanism most certainly offers.

Chapter II

Cultural and Agenda Conflicts in Academia: Critical Issues for Africana[1] Women's Studies

Well, chillum, whar dar is so much racket, dar must be something out o' kilter. I t'ink dat 'twixt de niggers of de Souf [both men and women] an' de women at de Norf' all a—talkin' bout rights, de white men will be n a fix pretty soon. But what's all dis here talkin' about? Dat man ober dar say dat women needs to be helped into carriages, and lifted ober ditches, and to have de best place everywhere....Nobody eber helped me into carriages, or ober mud puddles, or give me any best place! And aren't I a Woman? [The issue is her blackness-and-race not her womanhood that has caused her to be excluded.] Look at me. Look at my arm. I have plowed and planted and gathered into barns and not man could head me—and aren't I a woman? I have born'd five children and seen 'em mos' all sold off into slavery, and when I cried out with mother's grief, none but Jesus heard...and aren't I a woman? Den dey talks 'bout dis t'ing in de head—what dis dey call it? Dat's it, honey—intellect....Now, What's dat got to do wit women's rights or niggers' rights [two separate groups who share the common-ality of oppression]? If my cup won't hold but a pint and yourn holds a quart, wouldn't ye be mean not to let me have my little half-measure full? Den dat little

> man in black dar, he say women can't have as much
> rights as man, 'cause Christ warn't a woman….Whar
> did your Christ come from? Whar did your Christ
> come from? From God and a woman! Man had noth-
> ing to do with him! If de fust woman God ever made
> was strong enough to turn the world upside down, all
> alone—dese togedder ought to be able to turn it back
> and get it rightside up again; and now dey is asking
> to do it, de men better let 'em. Bleeged to ye for
> hearin' on me; and now ole Sojourner hain't got noth-
> ing more to say. (Truth, 104)

During her lifetime as a staunch upholder of truth and justice, Sojourner Truth, born a slave in 1797 and freed under the 1827 New York Sate Emancipation Act, often unexpectedly appeared at antislavery and women's rights rallies. Her impromptu remarks often-times served to refute antagonistic arguments against both her race and her sex—and in that order. Her frequently quoted speech above, which was both unso-licitedly delivered and, because of her color, initially unwelcomed by the white audience at an 1852 Woman's Rights Convention in Akron, Ohio, is used here to demonstrate the critical position of the Africana woman within the context of the modern feminist movement.

Historically, Africana women have fought against sexual discrim-ination, as well as race and class discrimination; they have, indeed, chal-lenged Africana male chauvinism, but not to the extent of eliminating Africana men as allies in the struggle for liberation and familihood. To be sure, historically, Africana women have wanted to be "liberated" to the community, family, and its responsibilities; for the evacuation of males and females in the Africana community from nine to five has alarmingly reeked havoc on the sense of security of Africana children left behind in that community. Consequently, in the absence of parental guidance and discipline, gangs, often become the substitute parent. But somehow over the years, the distress of and need for comforting Africana children seem to have been ignored, overlooked, and vastly underplayed, suggesting that these children do not require this kind of support. The result is generations of hurt and rejection. Even Africana women, who happen to be on welfare and are perhaps at home, are con-demned for not having a job and thus are often regarded as negative figure sin the sense that they do not offer an adult presence. With polarized minds, Africanans have bought into this view, embracing all too frequently the stereotype of the Africana woman on welfare and the disapproval of it. Nevertheless, Africana women are seeking to reclaim security, stability, and nurturing of a family-based community. According to Vivian Gordon:

> To address women's issues, therefore, is not only to address the crucial needs of Black women, it is also to address the historic primacy of the African and African American community; that is, the primacy of its children and their preparation for the responsibilities and privileges of mature personhood.[3] [*Black Women, Feminism and Black Liberation: Which Way?* viii]

Hence, Africana women have historically demonstrated that they are diametrically opposed to the concept of many white feminists who want independence and freedom from family responsibilities. In the Statement of Purpose that the National Organization of Women (NOW) issued in 1966 and still issues today, "…it is no longer either necessary or possible for women to devote the greater part of their lives to child rearing…."[2] Apparently, the motivating factor of many of these women is the desire to be liberated from the family. Others take it a step farther in their desire to be liberated from the obligation to men in particular; this sentiment, of course, may appeal more to radical lesbian or to radical feminist separatists. It is too often the case that many white feminists deny traditional familihood as a paramount part of their personal and professional lives.

All too frequently, Sojourner's resounding query "And aren't I a woman?" is extrapolated from the text in order to force feminist identification on the speaker without any initial or even later reference to her first obstacle, race. In fact, as indicated on the occasion of Sojourner's speech, white's had not even deemed her as human, let alone as a woman, which is precisely why she was mocked before they finally allowed her to speak. One may question what this has to do with the modern feminist movement? The fact is that these racist perceptions have not changed significantly enough to suggest that Africana women do not yet have to contend with the same problem of insidious racism with almost equal intensity even though it is somewhat masked today.

In attempting to unearth historical truths about the feminist movement that divide white feminists from black feminists, Hazel V. Carby asserts:

> In order to gain a public voice as orators or published writers, black women had to confront the dominant domestic ideologies and literary conventions of womanhood which exclude them from the definition "woman." (Carby, 6)

Moreover, many have farcically used Sojourner's quotation to justify labeling this freedom fighter as a feminist or a "prefeminist." White feminists often impose their interpretation of the Africana experience when it is convenient; for them, Sojourner's experience became a dramatization of female oppression. Ironically, Sojourner was attacking rather than embracing an element of the women's rights agenda that excluded her. Instead of aligning herself with the feminist cause, she was engaging in self-actualization, forcing white feminists, in particular, to recognize her and all Africana women as women and as a definite and legitimate part of that community. Furthermore, she was politically critiquing and defining herself and her movement. During the abolitionist movement white women learned techniques from the Africana women that would enable them to organize, to hold public meetings, and to conduct petition campaigns. As abolitionists, the white women first learned to speak in public and then began to formulate a philosophy to manifest their basic rights and their place in society. Africana women, on the other hand, had learned and practiced all these things centuries ago, from traditions in their Motherland.

But procrusteans have mislabeled Africana women activists like Sojourner Truth, along with other prominent Africana women freedom fighters such as Harriet Tubman (who spent her life aiding Africana slaves, both males and females, in their escape through the Underground Railroad to the North for freedom), and Ida B. Wells (an anti-lynching rebel during the early twentieth century) simply because they were women. Indeed, their primary concerns were not of a feminist nature but rather of a commitment to the centrality of the African-American freedom struggle. Their primary concern was the life-threatening plight of all Africana people, both men and women, at the hands of a racist system. To cast them in the feminist mold, which de-emphasizes their major concerns, is, in this writer's opinion, an abomination and an insult to the level of their audacious struggle and intent.

The problem is that too many Africanans have taken the theoretical framework of "feminism" and have tried to make it fit their particular circumstance. Rather than create their own paradigm, naming and defining themselves, some Africana women scholars, in particular, are persuaded by White feminists to adopt or to adapt to the white concept and terminology of feminism. The real benefit of the amalgamation of black feminism and white feminism goes to white feminists who can increase their power base by expanding their scope with the convenient consensus that sexism is their commonality and primary concern. They make a gender analysis of African-American life only to equate racism with sexism. Politically and ideologically for Africana women, such an adoption is misguided and simplistic. Most Africanans do not share the same ideology with traditional white feminists. True, the two may share strategies for ending sexual discrimination, but they are divided on the methodology to change the entire political system that would end racial discrimination and sexual exploitation. While the white feminist has not sacrificed her major concern, sexism, the "black feminist" has, in that she has yielded her primary concerns for racism and classism as secondary and tertiary issues. The modified terminology, "Black Feminism," is some black women's futile attempt to fit into the constructs of an established white female paradigm. At best, black feminism may relate to sexual discrimination outside the Africana community, but cannot claim to resolve the critical problems within the Africana community that are influenced by racism and classism. White feminist Bettina Aptheker accurately analyzes the problem:

> When we place women at the center of our thinking, we are going about the business of creating an historical and cultural matrix from which women may claim autonomy and independence over their own lives. For women of color, such autonomy cannot be achieved in conditions of racial oppression and cul-

> tural genocide....In short, "feminist," in the modern
> sense, means the empowerment of women. For
> women of color, such an equality, such an empow-
> erment, cannot take place unless the communities in
> which they live can successfully establish their own
> racial and cultural integrity. (Aptheker, 13)

For many white women, Africana women exist for their purpose—a dramatization of oppression. As for their identity, they define them-selves as the definitive woman. There is no need, for example, to name their studies "White" Women Studies. Moreover, while gender-spe-cific discrimination is the key issue for Women's Studies, it unfortunately narrows the goals of Africana liberation and devalues the quality of Africana life. Thus, it neither identifies nor defines the primary issue for Africana women or other women of color. Therefore, it is crucial that Africana women engage in self-naming and self-definition, lest they fall into the trap of refining a critical ideology at the risk of sur-rendering the critical self.

Africana women might begin by naming and defining their unique movement Africana womanism. Womanism can be traced back to Sojourner's speech, which begins to develop and highlight Africana women's unique experience into a paradigm of Africana women. In refining this terminology into a theoretical framework and method-ology, Africana womanism, while it identifies the participation and the role of Africana women in the struggle it does not suggest that female subjugation is the most critical issue they face in their struggle for parity. Like the so-called black feminism, Africana womanism acknowledges gender problems in society as a critical one that must be resolved; however, it views feminism, the suggested alternative to the problem, as a sort of inverted white patriarchy, with the white femi-nist now in command and on top. In other words, mainstream femi-nism is women's co-opting themselves into main-stream patriarchal values. According to Gordon:

> The Movement fails to state clearly that the system is
> wrong; what it does communicate is that White
> women want to be a part of the system. They seek
> power, not change. [Gordon, 47]

The Africana womanist, on the other hand, perceives herself as the companion to the Africana man and works diligently toward continuing their established union in the struggle against racial oppression. Within the Africana culture, there is that intrinsic, organic equality that was necessary for survival of the Africana culture, in spite of the individual personal problems of female subjugation infiltrating the family structure by the white male cultural system. This issue must be addressed. However, the white male's privilege is not the personal problem of the Africana man or woman; rather it is a political problem of unchallenged gender chauvinism in the world. Critiquing Women's Studies, Aptheker concludes that:

> women's studies programs operate within a racist structure. Every department in every predominantly white institution is centered on the experience, history, politics, and culture of white men, usually of the elite. What is significant, however, is that women's studies, by its very reason for existence, implies a reordering of politics, a commitment to community, and an educational purpose which is inherently subversive of its institutional setting....Insofar as women's studies replicates a racial pattern in which white rule predominates, however, it violates its own principles of origin and purpose. More to the point: it makes impossible the creation of a feminist vision and politics. [Aptheker, 13]

Africanans have more critical and complex problems in their community, and the source of these problems lies in racial oppression. Moreover, the Africana woman acknowledges the problem of classism, too, likewise a reproachable element in American's capitalistic system. However, even there—in the plight of the middle-class Africana women—it becomes intertwined with racism. Given that both the Africana womanist and the black feminist treat these same critical issues and more, there must be something that makes them different, and that something is prioritizing on the part of the Africana woman. She realizes the critical need to prioritize the antagonistic forces as racism, classism, and sexism respectively. In the final analysis, Africana womanism is connected to the tradition of being self-reliant and autonomous, working toward participation in Africana liberation.

Observe the importance of Africana identity in the scenario of Sojourner Truth for example. Before one can properly address her much-quoted query, one must, as she did, first address her color, for it was because of color that Sojourner Truth was initially hissed and jeered at for having the gall to presume that she should have a voice on the matter of any conflict between the men and the women and on the rights of the latter. Before Sojourner Truth could hope to address gender problems, she had to first overcome the problem of color for whites. Clearly, gender was not the salient issue for her. The need to reiterate "And Aren't I a Woman?" suggests Sojourner was insisting that she, too, possessed all the traits of a woman, notwithstanding her race and class, which the dominate culture used to exclude her from the community. Hence, the key issue for the Africana woman, as well as for the Africana man, is racism, with classism intertwined therein.

While the point is well taken that women of all ethnic orientations share the unfortunate commonality of female subjugation, it is naive, to say the least, to suggest that this kind of oppression should be the primary concern of all women, particularly women of color. When the black feminist buys the white terminology, she also buys its agenda. As Africana women share other forms of oppression that are not necessarily a part of the overall white women's experiences, their varied kinds of victimization need to be prioritized. Instead of alienating the Africanan male sector from the struggle today, Africanans must call for a renegotiation of Africanan male-female roles in society. In so doing, there must be a call to halt female subjugation once and for all, while continuing the crucial struggle for the liberation of Africana people the world over.

The notion of Africana women moving "from margin to center"[3] of the feminist movement, as proposed by black feminist Bell Hooks (who does a very good job in documenting the revolutionary role of Africana women in the abolitionist struggle) is ludicrous. For how can Africana women hope to move from the peripheral to the center of a movement that, historically, did not have her on the agenda? Even during the resurgence of the women's liberation movement of the mid-1960s, the critical concerns of the Africana woman was not on the agenda. In spite of this factor, Hooks complains that contemporary black women do not join together for women's rights because they do not see womanhood as an important aspect of their identity. Further, Hooks complains that racist and sexist socialization has conditioned black women to devalue their femaleness and to regard race as their only relevant label of identity. In short, she surmises that black women were asked to deny a part of themselves, and they did. Clearly this position evokes some controversy, as it does not take into account the dynamics of the Africana woman's reluctance to embrace feminism.

This writer is reminded of an experience a colleague had observed: From so many feet away, her race was noticed; as she moved into close proximity, her class was detected; but it was not until she got in the door that her sex was known. Does that not suggest the need for prioritization? Hence for Sojourner Truth, as for all Africana women, the first and foremost issue remains race, with class and sex following closely. Granted, the Africana woman does have additional battles to fight, for as history has revealed, her peculiar predicament within the dominant culture is that of a tripartite victim of racism, classism, and sexism.

Prioritizing the kinds of relegation to which the Africana woman is subjected should be explored in a serious effort to recognize and to understand the existence of her total sense of oppression. What one really wants to do is to appreciate the triple plight of Africana women. Society must deal with all aspects of the Africana woman's oppression in order to better combat them. Moreover, as the problems of race and then class, are the key societal issues for people of color, they must be resolved first if there is any hope for human survival. It is impossible to conceive of any human being succumbing to absolute regression without an outright struggle against it.

Sojourner Truth demonstrated early on in the women's rights movement that the commonality is betwixt the Africanans of the South (both men and women) in their struggle for freedom and the women of the North. Clearly, the Africana woman had no exclusive claim on the struggle for equal rights apart from her male counterpart. Africana men and Africana women are and should be allies, struggling as they have since slavery for equal social, economic, and political rights as fellow human beings in the world. There is an inherent contradiction in the ideology of "black feminism" that should be reevaluated. A more compatible terminology and concept is "Africana womanism."

Indeed, this issue must be properly addressed if Women's Studies is to be truly respected and if a positive agenda for African Women's Studies is to be truly realized.

Chapter III

Africana Womanism: The Authentic Agenda for Women of African Descent

Women authors are frequently still being ignored by male critics or put into a separate category as "feminist" which means that their works are not evaluated in the same way as those of male authors. My novels are not feminist; they are part of the corpus of African literature and should be discussed as such. . . . I deal with a variety of topics in my novels which are certainly not feminist: war, colonialism and the exploitation of Africa by the West, and many others. . . . I have not been relating well with Western feminists and have found myself at loggerheads with them from time to time. They are only concerned with issues that are related to themselves and transplant these onto Africa. . . . Western feminists are often concerned with peripheral topics and do not focus their attention on major concerns. . . . They think that by focusing on exotic issues in the "third world" they have internationalized their feminism. [Emecheta 50]

This is Buchi Emecheta, internationally acclaimed Nigerian novelist whose *The Joys of Motherhood* celebrates the pleasures women derive from fulfilling their responsibilities to their families concerning family matters such as child bearing, mothering, and nurturing, issues that are traditionally unpopular with mainstream feminists. The quotation comes from a 1980s interview Ravell Pinto conducted with the author at Spelman College in Atlanta, Georgia, where she denounced feminism as a theoretical construct for analyzing her works. Her comments are pertinent to black women in general, particularly in reference to the question of modern-day feminism, its relevancy and applicability to the lives and families of Africana women (i.e., African women and women of the African diaspora) worldwide.

The crucial question for the Africana woman today include: What is feminism? How does its origin, its agenda, and its leadership relate to the authentic Africana woman, particularly regarding both her and her entire community's historical and cultural realities? Generally speaking, the most pervasive gender-based methodology inside of the academy, feminism, is a theoretical construct named and defined by women of European descent whose primary goal is that of female empowerment, insisting upon female centrality, the very foundation upon which the feminist agenda and thought rest. As part of its agenda of female empowerment, feminism calls for women's insistence upon "breaking silence" or "finding voice" while justifying their movement from the home place to the work place. Thus, as Betty Friedan protests in *The Feminist Mystique*, "We can no longer ignore that voice within women that says, 'I want something more than my husband and my children and my home'" (27). The experiences, and hence, the agenda of Africana women, are polar opposite to those of white women, as the experiences of the latter contradict the needs and the demands of the former. According to renown Ghanian writer, Ama Ata Aidoo,

> For most West African women, work is a responsibility and an obligation. This idea is drummed into us from infancy. We never have had to fight for the "right to work"—a major concern of early Western feminists. In West Africa, virtually no family tolerates a woman who doesn't work. Consequently, there are not many homes in the region today . . . in which girls are discouraged from having ambitions of their own on the premise that they will marry and be looked after by men. [Aidoo 46]

As African men and women are co-rulers in what Zulu Sofola terms as "the dual-sex-system of socio-political power sharing fully," they actualize a legacy of long-standing communalism so characteristic of an authentic African worldview (Sofola 53-54). Again, the African woman, her role and opinions, are critical to the overall community. As Kamene Okonjo asserts, "The African woman has not been inactive, irrelevant and silent. Rather African tradition has seen the wisdom of a healthy social organization where all its citizens are seen to be vital channels for a healthy and harmonious society" [Okonjo 45].

Because feminism informs the ordering of issues revolving around the exclusivity of womanhood, it poses some serious problems for the Africana woman, particularly one who is not a black feminist. As proper naming is so critical to existence and meaning, one must be ever cognizant of all of its inherent denotations and connotations. Hence, the black feminist, by definition and by extension of the concept of the feminist, in view of the very name, aligns herself with the (white) feminist, even though she proposes to treat race and class issues along with the issue of gender simultaneously. Contrary to this claim of simultaneity in addressing race, class, and gender issues for the black feminist, according to Patricia Liggins Hill, a close look at the black feminist's activities reveals that "most of her energies go into the gender question" as a top priority (Hill 1378). With the exception of African feminism, which demonstrates only a misnaming, as "it is more closely akin to Africana womanism" in both agenda and priorities, the overall meaning of feminism holds true for any type of feminisms, beginning with mainstream feminism, which is defined by Filomina Chioma Steady as Bourgeois Feminism (Hudson-Weems, *Africana Womanism* 18). According to Steady, the bourgeois feminist "fails to deal with the major problem of equitable distribution of resources to all socioeconomic groups. Such an approach leads to a concentration of energies on sexual symbolism rather than on more substantive economic realities" (Steady, *The Black Woman* 24). Other feminisms include the cultural feminist, who focuses more on the application of a cultural critique like Marxism, "the liberal feminist, [who] tend [s] to join, rather than question, the White male-dominated power system itself and the radical feminist [who] acknowledges the differences between the males and females, but sees the two as antagonistic and in conflict"(Hudson-Weems, *Africana Womanism* 44).

Africana womanism, on the other hand, is an endemic paradigm, separate and distinct from all other female-based perspectives:

> Neither an outgrowth nor an addendum to femi-
> nism, *Africana Womanism* is not Black feminism,
> African feminism, or Walker's womanism that some
> Africana women have come to embrace. *Africana
> Womanism is* an ideology created and designed for all
> women of African descent. It is grounded in African
> culture, and therefore, it necessarily focuses on the
> unique experiences, struggles, needs, and desires of
> Africana women. It critically addresses the dynamics
> of the conflict between the mainstream feminist, the
> Black feminist, the African feminist, and the Africana
> womanist. The conclusion is that *Africana Womanism*
> and its agenda are unique and separate from both
> White feminism and Black feminism, and moreover,
> to the extent of naming in particular, *Africana
> Womanism* differs from African feminism. [Hudson-
> Weems, *Africana Womanism* 24]

Since prioritizing race, class, and gender frames the differentiation between them and black feminists, as well as white feminists for Africana women, it becomes clear, as Bettina Aptheker recognizes, that the first line of order for black women and their communities is to "establish their own racial and cultural integrity" (Aptheker quoted in *African Womanism*, 13). The recognition of the differences in the specific struggle of white women against white male domination, both inside and outside of their private domain, and black women in a concerted liberation struggle with their male counterparts becomes crucial.

Linda LaRue, stating her position some five years before Aptheker, understood this varying degree of white male domination relative to black men and women verses white women: "Blacks are oppressed and that means unreasonably burdened, unjustly, severely, rigorously, cru-elly and harshly fettered by white authority. White women, on the other hand, are only suppressed, and that means checked, restrained, excluded from conscious and overt activity. And this is a difference" (218).

Taking LaRue's concept to yet another level eight years later is Audre Lorde, who warned us of the dynamics of the discriminating phenomenon of black women/white women, black women/black men, and black/white interrelationships. This is particularly the case wherein black women erroneously accept the notion that they have a shared commonality with white women as being equally subjugated by their male counterparts, which is a commentary on how the psyche of black women, who buy into this notion, can negatively impact on the black community. Rather than have a shared oppression with white women, black women share oppression with black men in society:

> Black women and white women are not the same. For example, it is easy for Black women to be used by the power structure against Black men, not because they are men, but because they are Black. Therefore, for Black women, it is necessary at all times to separate the needs of the oppressor from our own legitimate conflicts within our communities. This same problem does not exist for white women. Black women and men have shared racist oppression and still share it.... Out of that shared oppression we have developed joint defenses and joint vulnerabilities to each other that are not duplicated in the white community. [Lorde 118]

This phenomenon of "shared racist oppression" is dramatized in Morrison' *Beloved*, which Hudson-Weems explores in *Africana Womanism*:

> Sethe and Paul D. unquestionably share a common bond, as "her story was bearable because it was his as well—to tell, to refine and tell again" (99). They have both been victimized in similar ways—both used as work horses and abused as grantees of the sexual whims of their oppressors. As readers are well aware the women in *Beloved* represent the victims of "the 'unspeakable' fate to which most female slaves were heiresses," so are readers aware that this fate is one not experienced by the slave woman alone (Samuels and Hudson-Weems 94). On the contrary, Africana men, too, experienced sexual exploitation by their slave-holders, thereby validating this author's thesis

that sexual exploitation and racism more closely identify the dynamics of the Africana experience during
slavery than does the notion of sexual exploitation
and gender. (124)

That said, one should not conclude that the gender factor is not
an important issue for the black woman. Quite the contrary, the Africana
woman, too, trapped in a patriarchal society, must consciously address
the gender question, which she can only realistically do after dealing
with race. This prerequisite is also the order for first dealing with the
question of class, which many Africanans, in areas of the world where
they are in the vast majority, believe to be the most critical issue. Even
in these areas, including the Caribbean, where African Caribbeans
believe that, as a black dominated society, economic equality is their
number one concern, in reality it is racism that dictates their level of
existence, thereby prohibiting economic parity for them as an oppressed
group. This is true in South Africa as well, where as late as the mid-
nineties, as noted by South African activist Ruth Mompati, her country was the only one in the world where racism continued to be a
legal institution under the system of apartheid. Here again the reality
attests to the fact that even in a predominantly black country on the
black continent of Africa, the societal order of black inferiority is
informed by the racist power structure of white supremacy. Thus, it is
not happenstance that economic power, even in these areas, resides
among the so-called dominant culture.

Historically and currently, both Black men and women work
together, collectively, toward realizing liberation and equality. In reflecting on the beginnings of the American experience for the majority
of Africans in the United States since 1619, I can say that some progress
has been made. The struggles of the seventeenth to the mid-nineteenth
centuries culminated in the Civil War (1861-1865) and the signing of
the Emancipation Proclamation in 1863, which granted blacks legal
freedom from physical bondage. Its aftermath, for the remaining of
that century, was characterized by the continuing struggle against abject
servitude, demonstrated in the Post-Civil War milieu of Reconstruction
and Jim Crowism. At the turn of the twentieth century African
Americans continued in the struggle against racial discrimination, particularly with W.E.B. DuBois' insistence upon not only civil rights,

but on our right to vote and on our right to an equal education as outlined in his classic, *The Souls of Black Folk.* Those interests carried us into the fifties and the sixties, the defining years of the Civil Rights era, which culminated in the signing of the civil rights Bill in 1964. Since that monumental event, African Americans have been oscillating, believing that we have arrived and at the same time questioning the true meaning of civil rights for us who are still treated, both overtly and covertly, as second-class citizens in many instances. With the knowledge that racism continues to rear its ugly head, having no intentions on the part of the dominant culture of surrendering the awesome phenomenon of white supremacy, it should be clear that the only way that Africanans can hope to rise up out of this dilemma is through a collective struggle of both men and women against the odds of racist inequality.

It is even more clear that we as a people cannot afford to divide our energies and concerns along the popular gender line of feminism, so characteristic of the contemporary battle between the sexes within the dominant culture. Sociologist Delores Aldridge, in her *Focusing: Black Male-Female Relationships,* cautions us against this, seeing it as a derailing of our liberation struggle: "One might argue . . . that the women's liberation—as it is presently defined and implemented—has a negative impact on the black liberation movement . . . [for] women's liberation operates within the capitalist tradition and accepts the end goals of sexist white males" (Aldridge 35). With this in mind, it becomes critically necessary for oppressed people to establish who they are and what their struggle need be for survival. Moreover, it is equally important to establish the true role of the Africana woman as a non-participant in a separate struggle from her male counterpart as does the feminist, but rather as co-partner with the Africana man in this humongous struggle between the races. Frederick Douglass, as reflected in his opinions on women's rights, understood this well:

> I have always championed women's rights to vote; but it will be seen that the present claim of the Negro is the one of the most urgent necessity. The assertion of the right of woman to vote meets nothing but ridicule. There is no deep-seated malignity in the hearts of the people against her; but name the right

of the Negro to vote, all hell is turned loose and the Ku Klux and Regulators hunt and slay the unoffending black man. The government of this country loves women. They are the sisters, mothers, wives, and daughters of our rulers. [84]

In the 1997 article "Africana Womanism and the Critical Need for Africana Theory and Thought"—the seed for *Contemporary Africana Theory and Thought* of which I am editor, using black female models of our past during slavery, I discuss the legacy of the collective role of Africana women in the on going liberation struggle:

> Further emphasizing the race factor was [activist] Maria W. Stewart, who, two decades before [Sojourner] Truth's famous oration [1852], expanded the same work of Black cultural nationalism in 1831 by emphasizing the leadership role that Black women must play in the Black liberation struggle, thereby picking up where [activist] David Walker left off before his [1831] untimely and mysterious death, with his emphasis on Black male leadership in the liberation struggle. This pre-Africana womanist [Maria Stewart] "advised . . . Black women to unite to express and further develop their full potential as women and as culture bearers. Speaking before the African-American Female Intelligence Society, she charges Black women with the survival and enrichment of the Black community." [83]

A poignant example of the primacy of family and the need for prioritizing human dignity and racial parity is told in a story by jMompati, who relates her experience of going into a large auditorium and witnessing countless decomposed bodies of children who had become victims of apartheid:

> The South African woman [situation described above], finds the order of her priorities in her struggle for human dignity and her rights as a woman dic-

tated by the general political struggle of her people as a whole. The national liberation of the Black South African is a prerequisite to her own liberation and emancipation as a woman and a worker. [112-13]

To be sure, this quotation is a firm representation of the opinion of Daphne Ntiri, an astute African scholar who specializes in women's issues. She contends that "human discrimination transcends sex discrimination. . . . the costs of human suffering are high when compared to a component, sex obstacle" (Ntiri 6). Echoing that idea is Filomina Chioma Steady in *The Black Woman Cross-Culturally*, who holds that

for the black woman in a racist society, racial factors, rather than sexual ones, operate more consistently in making her a target for discrimination and marginalization. This becomes apparent when the "family" is viewed as a unit of analysis. Regardless of differential access to resources by both men and women, white males and females, as members of family groups, share a proportionately higher quantity of the earth's resources than do black males and females. There is a great difference between discrimination by privilege and protection, and discrimination by deprivation and exclusion. [27-28]

Here her assessment addresses the source of discrimination that Africana women continue to endure. According to Hudson-Weems:

There is the oppression of the South African woman who must serve as maid and nurse to the White household with minimum wage earnings, the Caribbean woman in London who is the ignored secretary, and the Senegalese or African worker in France who is despised and unwanted. There is the Nigerian subsistence farmer, such as the lbo woman in Enugu and Nsukka, who farms every day for minimum wages, and the female Brazilian factory worker who is the lowest on the totem pole. Clearly, the problems of these women are not inflicted upon them solely because they are women. They are victimized first and foremost because they are Black; they are further victimized because they are women living in a male-dominated society. [*Africana Womanism* 30]

The problems of Africana women, including physical brutality, sexual harassment, and female subjugation in general, perpetrated both within and beyond the Africana community, must ultimately be resolved on a collective basis within their communities. Because "Africana men have unfortunately internalized the White patriarchal system to some degree," they must first come together with their female counterparts and work toward eliminating racist influences in their lives, with the realization that no form of subjugation, female subjugation included, can be allowed to exist (Hudson-Weems, *Africana Womanism* 63). Along those same lines, Ntiri summarizes Mompati's position that sexism "is basically a secondary problem which arises out of race, class and economic prejudices" (quoted in *Africana Womanism* 5). Although Steady fails to properly name herself, she does, however, demonstrate a strong sense of priorities in the following quotation, clearly in alignment with the sense of prioritizing race issues inherent in Africana womanism:

Regardless of one's position, the implications of the feminist movement for the black woman are complex.... Several factors set the black woman apart as having a different order of priorities. She is oppressed not simply because of her sex but ostensibly because of her race and, for the majority, essentially because of their class. Women belong to different socio-economic groups and do not represent a universal category. Because the majority of black women are poor, there is likely to be some alienation from the middle-class aspect of the women's movement that perceives feminism as an attack on men rather than on a system which thrives on inequality. [Steady, *The Black Woman* 23-24]

In her article in *Women in Africa and the African Diaspora,* she further asserts:

> For the majority of black women poverty is a way of life. For the majority of black women also racism has been the most important obstacle in the acquisition of the basic needs for survival. Through the manipulation of racism the world economic institutions have produced a situation which negatively affects black people, particularly black women. What we have, then, is not a simple issue of sex or class differences but a situation which, because of the racial factor, is castlike in character on both a national and global scale. [Steady, "African Feminism" 18-19]

Focusing on the question of class in the Africana woman's experience, it goes hand in hand with the question of race. Clearly, from an historical perspective slavery was synonymous with poverty. When one examines the origin of American racism, one realizes that it was an attitude constructed to authorize economic exploitation by the dominant culture in order to acquire free or cheap labor. It became more of a race issue when proslavery advocates attempted to rationalize this economic exploitation, arguing race inferiority as a justification for slavery. Hence, racism and classism are inextricable. It should be noted, however, that since the legal emancipation of Africanans, racism has become a bigger monster than classism, even though the latter is the parent of the former. As this issue relates to the Africana woman, Steady makes the following assessment in *The Black Woman Cross-Culturally*:

> The issue of black women's oppression and racism are part of the "class issue," but there is a danger of subsuming the black woman's continued oppression to class and class alone. For even within the same class there are groups that are more oppressed than others. Blacks are likely to experience hardship and discrimination more severely and consistently than whites, because of racism. [Steady, *The Black Woman* 26]

From the beginning it has been apparent that Africana women in particular have been and must continue to be concerned with prioritizing the obstacles in this society, i.e., the lack of equal access to career
opportunities, fair treatment of their children, and equal employment
for their male counterparts. Long before questions of gender and class
came to the forefront in contemporary literary criticism and theoretical constructs, positions were taken and decisions were made about
options available to the Africana woman on the basis of her race. Thus,
it was and remains evident that the Africana woman must first fight
the battle of racism.

In reflecting exclusively on the question of gender for the Africana
woman, it is naive for Africana women to believe that whenever they
address gender issues, they are engaging in feminist activity, and hence,
because gender problems are serious issues for them too, they see themselves as needing feminism as a means of confronting this concern. In
fact, some Africana scholars take it a step further, claiming that they
are the "original feminists," insisting that black women were feminists
long before "feminism," as if the term itself is so inherently sacred that
they must be identified or connected with it. They vow that they will
not let white women have feminism, herein engaging in a ludicrous
battle for turf that clearly does not belong to them, turf many black
women insist that they do not need anyway for various reasons. Be
that as it may, Africana womanism, necessarily addresses gender issues,
which does not translate into mandating one's identification with or
one's dependency upon feminism/black feminism as the only viable
means of addressing them.

Feminism, an agenda designed to meet the needs and demands of
white women, is plausible for that group, with its victims of gender
oppression primarily. They are within their rights to tailor a theoretical construct for the purpose of addressing their need to eradicate
female subjugation first. However, placing all women's history under
white women's history, thereby assigning the definitive position to the
latter, is highly problematic, for it demonstrates the ultimate in racial
arrogance in so far as it suggests that authentic activity of women in
general resides with white women. It is, therefore, ludicrous to pro-
claim as feminists such Africana women activists and writers as Maria
Stewart and Frances Watkins Harper, leading abolitionists; Sojourner
Truth, militant abolition spokesperson and universal suffragist; Harriet

Tubman, Underground Railroad conductor; Ida B. Wells, early twentieth-century antilynching crusader; and even to some degree, Anna Julia Cooper, who at least acknowledges in *A Voice from the South* that "woman's cause is man's cause: [We] rise or sink together, dwarfed or godlike, bond or free" (61). Moreover, Mary Church Terrell, president of the National Association of Colored Women, asserted that "Not only are colored women ... handicapped on account of their sex, but they are almost everywhere baffled and mocked because of their race. Not only because they are women, but because they are colored women" (Freeman 531). The assertions here strongly anticipate that of African Nigerian activist Taiwo Ajai a century later, who holds that Africana women's "emancipation is unattainable until the basic rights are provided all [black] people" (62-3).

Be that as it may, while Julia Hare rejects the terminology "black feminism" for black women's movement, "Black Feminism is not a word that describes the plight of Black women," black feminists reject black non-feminists and their collective agenda of, say, Africana womanism, which they may feel offers competition for their concept, particularly since many black women accepted feminism/black feminism for lack of an alternative paradigm (Hare 15). Often appropriating parts of the paradigm of Africana womanism and attempting to reshape it referring to it as "new black feminism," Hortense Spillers, who introduced in the 2000 DuBois Conference in Philadelphia, insists that black women need feminism in order to address the gender question. Again this is not true, as the feminist has no exclusive on gender issues. Seemingly the new black feminist believes embracing Africana womanism would automatically mean invalidating their years of black feminist interpretations; rather they should view it as an evolutionary process of ideological growth and development. Womanism is a terminology only introduced and not fully developed by author Alice Walker, since creating theory lies outside her literary activities as novelist, short story writer, poet, and essayist. Black women scholars have since taken up Walker's terminology and proceeded to shape a paradigm for it, even though much of what they outlined as womanist theory had already been outlined as black womanist/Africana womanist theory as early as the mid-eighties. Moreover, white feminists, too, have begun to revise and appropriate parts of Africana womanism, as demonstrated in their new emphasis on including men in their dialogue; whereas, earlier they had fought to exclude them from their dialogue as a means of debating and of possibly changing the antagonistic forces of white male domination. To be sure, the Africana womanist has always invited the male component:

> The critical concern here is how the problem is to be resolved, with specific reference to the exclusion of the very instrument of female subjugation, the male, who, in the final analysis, obviously needs himself to be corrected and redeemed. Africana women, instead of addressing relational conflicts between Africana men and themselves by excluding the former, should work toward resolving the tension via working together with mutual respect. [Hudson-Weems, *Africana Womanism* 62]

While Nancy Caraway's mission to correct the lack of documentation regarding the historical role of black women in the feminist movement may very well be part of the motivation behind the Black Feminist Revisionist Project, the final possible explanation to it, as I perceive it, is the response of black feminists to Africana womanism. Engaging heavily in this one-sided practice, Black feminist revisionists, including Evelyn Brooks Higginbotham, who contends that "histories of Black women leaders and their organizations often play a double-revisionist role in as much as they reinterpret the revisionist works of White feminist historians," (255) as well as bell hooks, Patricia Hill-Collins, Beverly Guy Sheftall, Angela Davis, Jonetta B. Cole, etc., misclaim all noted black women and their works and activities as feminists on the basis of gender alone. Thus are called twentieth-century women freedom fighters like Ida B. Wells and Rosa Parks feminists. in much the same way as a white feminist like Caraway would do. Be that as it may, Iva Carruthers, however, rescued Parks in particular from the feminist arena years ago, in the early eighties:

> In the American experience the feminist movement had effectively displaced Black unity, whether in the context of the Abolitionist movement, the right-to-vote movement or the civil rights movement. And

so we sit idly by and let whites turn Harriet Tubman
and Rosa Parks into supporters of White feminism as
opposed to race defenders. (Carruthers 18)

The truth of the matter is that the majority of black women are
not feminist/black feminist, but rather they are black women activists
whose activities are best characterized by race-based activities as outlined by Africana womanism. From these early Africana women activis-
its and countless other unsung Africana heroines, white feminists have,
in reality, taken the lifestyle and techniques, to using them as blue-
prints to frame their theory. For example, black women have been
neither silent nor voiceless as seems to have been the case of feminists
in general who aspire to this quality; thus "breaking silence" and "finding voice" have become a major goal for them, while it has never been
a part of the authentic Africana woman's agenda,. In Betty Friedan's *The
Feminist Mystique,* she describes the feeling of disenchantment with
household drudgery on the part of white women and their desire to
be free, asserting that there is a:

> strange stirring, a sense of dissatisfaction, a yearning
> that women suffered in the middle of the twentieth
> century in the United States. Each suburban wife
> struggled with it alone as she made the beds, shopped
> for groceries, matched slipcover materials, ate peanut
> butter sandwiches with the children, chauffeured Cub
> Scouts and Brownies, lay beside her husband at
> night—she was afraid to ask even of herself the silent
> question—is this all? [Friedan 11]

This would hardly be the reaction of black women, who would readily respond that if this is all they could expect from the relationship, then
the relationship is in trouble.

The white woman, then, proceeded to name, define, and legit-
imize feminism as the only substantive women's movement. Thus, in
defining the feminist and her activities, they are identifying with inde-
pendent Africana women, whom they both emulated and despised—
dating back to slavery and extending into the searing sixties with the
modem civil rights movement—like Fannie Lou Hammer, Mamie

Till Mobley, and Rosa Parks. "Therefore, when Africana women come along and embrace feminism, appending it to their identity as Black feminists or African feminists, they are in reality duplicating the duplicate" (Hudson-Weems, *Africana Womanism* 22). Moreover, in her article "The African Feminist" Steady admits:

> Various schools of thought, perspectives, and ideological proclivities have influenced the study of feminism. Few studies have dealt with the issue of racism, since the dominant voice of the feminist movement has been that of the white female. The issue of racism can become threatening, for it identifies white feminists as possible participants in the oppression of blacks. [Steady, "The African Feminist" 3]

With these issues hovering over feminism's domain, the Africana community, by and large, has agreed that the feminist movement is the white women's movement for two reasons, while black women in the Academy futilely hold on to it as representative of their level of struggle. In spite of their over-all position in the Academy, Africana women, to begin with, do not view their male counterparts as their primary enemy as do white feminists, who are carrying out an age-old battle with their counterparts for subjugating them as property. According to Nigeria's first woman playwright, Zulu Sofola: "It [the dual-gender system between African men and women] is not a battle where the woman fights to clinch some of 'men's power.' Foreign cultures have both ignited and fueled a perpetual gender conflict that has now poisoned the erstwhile healthy social order of traditional Africa" (Sofola 62).

Moreover, contrary to the white feminists' need to be equal to men as human beings, black women have always been equal to their male counterparts, in spite of some Africana men's attempts to subjugate them on some levels. According to Angela Davis in *Women, Race and Class*:

> The salient theme emerging from domestic life in the [American] slave quarters is one of sexual equality. The labor that slaves performed for their own sake

48

and not for the aggrandizement of their masters was
carried out on terms of equality. Within the confines
of their family and community life, therefore, Black
people transformed that negative equality which
emanated from the equal oppression they suffered as
slaves into a positive quality: the egalitarianism characterizing their social relations. [18]

In addition, during American slavery, Africana women were as
harshly treated, physically and mentally, as were their male counterparts, thereby invalidating the alignment of Africana women and white
women as equals in the struggle. Indeed, the endless chores of the
Africana woman awaited her both in and outside the home. Africana
men and women have been equal partners in the struggle against
oppression from early on, again, unable to afford division based on
gender. Granted that, in some traditional societies, male domination
was/is a characteristic; but in the African–American slave experience,
Africana men and women in the same light viewed the slave owners
the same, thereby negating traditional (African or European) notions
of male or female roles.

Black sociologist, Joyce Ladner in *Tomorrow's Tomorrow* also comments on the black woman's opinion of the black man as not her primary enemy: "Black women do not perceive their enemy to be black
men, but rather the enemy is considered to be oppressive forces in the
larger society which subjugate black men, women and children" (277-
278). Therefore, the black man has no institutional power to oppress
Africana women or anyone else for that matter to the same degree as
white men do in the case of their women and people in general. In the
final analysis, the Africana "females and males were equal in the sense
that neither gender wielded economic power over the other" (Boulin
49). Given these realities, Germaine Greer's contention that "Men are
the enemy. They know it—at least they know there is a sex war on, an
unusually cold one…." appears inapplicable to the circumstance of
Africana women and the over-all Africana community (Lashmar 33).

Today, Africana women must insist that they are equal partners in
a relationship in which passive female subjugation neither was nor is
the norm in their community. According to Nobel Laureate, Toni
Morrison in "What the Black Woman Thinks about Women's Lib":

For years black women accepted that rage, even regarded that acceptance as their unpleasant duty. But in so doing they frequently kicked back, and they seem never to have become the true slaves that white women see in their own history" (63). Indeed, Africana women have not had that sense of powerlessness that white women speak of, nor have they been silenced or rendered voiceless by their male counterparts, as is the expressed experience of white women. The labels "black matriarch," "Sapphire," and "bitch" appended to the Africana woman to describe her personality and/or character clearly contradict the notion of the Africana woman as voiceless. Moreover, unlike the white woman, the Africana woman has been neither privileged nor placed on a pedestal for protection and support.

In conclusion, as I reflect on the embryonic stage of "Africana womanism" in the mid-eighties, which I earlier referred to as "black womanism," I found it necessary to name and define the true concerns, priorities, and activities of black women. As I participated in international dialogues at international conferences, serving on panels relative to Africana women and their true role within the constructs of the modern feminist movement, it became clear to me that Africana women globally, both in their private and public lives, engage in supporting their male counterparts as a number one priority to ensure the safety and security of their families and communities. Reflecting on the history of Africana people and women in particular, I concluded that for centuries Africana women have been engaging in Africana womanist activities, demonstrating the priority of race as collective activists, and that this inheritance dates back to the rich legacy of African womanhood. Thus, the existence of this phenomenon—Africana womanism—is not new, but rather a practice that dates back to Africa. To be sure, *Africana Womanism* takes its models from African women warriors and moves on to create a paradigm relative to this age-old legacy of Africana women activism. And so, in returning to the collective struggle and leadership of Africana people globally for the survival of our entire family/community, let us not forget our past strengths, indeed, the rich legacy of our glorious African ancestry, and indeed, the rich legacy of Africana womanhood.

Chapter IV

Proud Africana Women Activists: A Legacy of Strong, Family-Centered Culture Bearers

> An Africana woman . . . is a black woman activist who is family-centered rather than female centered and who focuses on race and class empowerment before gender empowerment. Of all the theoretical models, Hudson-Weems's best describes the racially based perspective of many black women's rights advocates, beginning with Maria W. Stewart and Frances Watkins Harper in the early nineteenth century. (Hill, *Call and Response*, 1979)

Central to the above quotation is the primacy of the centrality of family and the priority of race empowerment in the rich legacy of African womanhood and motherhood. Descending from a lineage of strong, proud African women activists and culture bearers, dating back to the advent of the colonization of Africa by Europe, notwithstanding African warrior queens in antiquity beginning with Queen Hatsphepsut (1505-1485 B.C.E.), whose "reign was one of the most outstanding in the 18th Dynasty of Egypt, proving that a woman can be a strong and effective ruler," the sixteenth century gives us the powerful Queen Nzingha (1583-1663) of Matamba, West Africa (Clarke 123-124). Nzingha, a powerful role model, demonstrate unquestionable persistence as an astute military strategist who fearlessly led her army of brave women warriors against Portuguese domination for forty years. The struggle continues for race empowerment on the continent of Africa, and in the nineteenth century, we witness Queen Mother Yaa Asantewa of Ejisu, Ghana, who bravely led the Ashanti people against the British colonialist in the Yaa Asantewa War. According to eminent Africanist John Henrik Clarke, Yaa Asantewa only added to that long line of African warrior queens who began with Hatshepsut fifteen hundred years before the birth of Christ. Because her agitation for the return of Prempeh[2] was converted into the stirring demands for independence, it is safe to say that she helped to create part of the theoretical basis for the political emergence of modern Africa (Clarke 133).

An African continuum of the race empowerment struggle as late as the nineteenth century in America, the last century of legalized American slavery, the struggle for the liberation of African people in America offers such noted nurturing female culture bearers as Sojourner Truth (1797-1883), abolitionist and women's rights crusader; Maria W. Stewart (1803-1879), abolitionist who carried on David Walker's legacy of self-determination and self-defense; Frances Watkins Harper (1824-1911), abolitionist and women's right advocate who declared that racism (even of her white sisters), and not black men, remained the greatest obstacle to black women's progress; and Harriet Tubman (1820-1913), Underground Railroad conductor who traveled to the South nineteen times to lead her fellow enslaved people—men, women and children—not just sisters, out of physical bondage.

Continuing to persevere and serve as strong, positive Africana women role models for future generations are Ida B. Wells (1869-1931), twentieth-century activists as antilynching crusader; Amy Ashwood Garvey (1897-1969), pan-Africanist and first wife of Marcus Garvey; Shirley Graham DuBois (1907-1977), pan-Africanist and wife of W.E.B. DuBois; Queen Mother Moore (1889-1998), staunch Garveyite and Republic of New Africa herald; Fannie Lou Hamer (1917-1977), grass roots warrior of Mississippi who helped to launch the Mississippi Freedom Democratic Party; Ella Baker (1903-1986), mother of the Student Non-Violent Coordinating Committee (SNCC); Rosa Parks (1913-), the established mother of the modern civil rights movement; Mamie Till Mobley (1921-), the mother of Emmett Louis "Bobo" Till, whose brutal lynching became the catalyst of the Modern Civil Rights Movement of the fifties and the sixties; Winnie Mandela (1936-), former wife of South African President Nelson Mandela, who continues her fight against apartheid even today, though it is on another level. And the list continues.

It must be noted that the role of the woman as liberation activist stems from her great love for and commitment to her personal family. According to Karen Anderson, "Women are extremely valuable in the sight of society. Not only do they bear life, but they nurse, they cherish, they give warmth, they care for life since all human life passes through their own bodies" (3).

Clearly we have a commitment to the lives of our own, and thus, the Africana womanist assumes her responsibility for her family with pleasure; it is impossible for her to separate her survival from that of her family. In a traditional Africana womanist fashion of adaptability, then, one of the eighteen characteristics of Africana womanism, the Africana womanist, unlike the feminist, who insists upon her "separate space," as Virginia Woolf called for in *A Room of One's Own*, stays connected to her family and participates in the collective liberation struggle, oftentimes assuming even leadership when needed, as did African queens of antiquity. Hence, as Akbar contends,

> The Africana–American woman would have to work on her historically adaptive role of assuming family leadership. There must be a greater willingness to share that leadership and in some instances to relinquish it. With both women and men using their historically earned strength of perseverance to deal with these historical adaptations, it becomes feasible to expect solutions. (53)

In fact, protecting her family, her children in particular, illustrates the high premium she places on family centrality, a critical component of Africana womanism. Lovingly and responsibly, the Africana woman is the mother of all humankind and thus, unquestionably the supreme mother nurturer.

> The Africana womanist is committed to the art of mothering and nurturing, her own children in particular and humankind in general. The collective role is supreme in Africana culture, for the Africana woman descends from a legacy of fulfilling the role of supreme

Mother Nature—nurturer, provider, and protector.
(Hudson-Weems, *Africana Womanism* 72)

Given the total picture of the Africana womanist, our past role models have proven to be strong, proud culture bearers; women who played a seminal, active role in the on going liberation struggle for Africana people worldwide. In concert with her male counterpart, she continues to share with her male counterpart the mission of bringing about total liberation for her people.

Notwithstanding the positive legacy of the Africana woman, the history of her struggle is a complex one. While she places the needs of her family before her own individual needs, she, too, has also fallen victim of patriarchy, as most women have.

> The history of the Africana woman reveals her peculiar predicament within the dominant culture as victim of a tripartite form of oppression—racism, classism, and sexism, respectively. Since American slavery, she and the Africana man have experienced much brutality; however, her womanhood has placed her in an even more vulnerable position. [Hudson-Weems, "The Tripartite Plight" 192]

This victimization of Africana women has unfortunately resulted in a current breakdown in our traditional lifestyle and values; for many have come to dismiss the need for prioritizing race and have instead opted to focus on gender issues. Be that as it may, however, in reassessing the true agenda of the Africana woman, one need only reflect on the urgency of family centrality and race priority as presented in the response of South African activist, Mompati, to the children victims of apartheid:

> The process of struggle for national liberation has been accompanied by the politicizing of both men and women. This has kept the women's struggle from generating into a sexist struggle that would divorce men's position in society from the political, social, and economic development of the society as a whole. From the South African women, who together with their

> men seek to liberate their country, comes an appeal
> to friends and supporters to raise their voices on their
> behalf. [Ntiri, *One is Not a Woman*, 112-113]

From this moving plea for the continuation of the collective struggle of African men, women, and children here, it is evident where the energies of this authentic Africana woman will go. It must be noted that long before Africa's colonialization, strong African women stood as equal partners with their male counterparts and operated within a cooperative, collective communal system. Coming from an agricultural-based economy, African men did not find it necessary to discriminate against their women, for in their situation, all shared in all aspects of life, labor included. This legacy was brought to America by the enslaved, as evidenced in Sojourner Truth's "And Aren't I a Woman?" which evokes Maria Stewart's resounding query nearly twenty years earlier, "What if I am a woman . . ." in her 1833 *Farewell Address to Her Friends in Boston*. Sojourner speaks to the equality of black men and women, even to the point of being equals in the work place: "I have plowed and planted and gathered into barns and no man could head me—and ain't I a woman?" (Truth, 104). Also echoing this phenomenon of egalitarianism are John Blassingame in *The Slave Community*, and Angela Davis in *Women, Race and Class*. In addition, Harriet Tubman's repeated efforts in rescuing her people with the realization that her freedom is interconnected with that of her brothers and sisters in bondage, convincingly demonstrate the primacy of combating racism with a sense of family and community commitment, a perspective handed down centuries ago by our African forebearers.

From slavery to freedom, the struggle continues for the fruition of true emancipation for Africana people. Moving from the advent of nineteenth-century legal freedom to twentieth-century slavery, it is not unreasonable to assert that Ida B. Wells was one of the bravest sisters of post Emancipation, particularly considering the danger of her efforts to expose in print the truth behind the myriad lynchings of black men resulting from the countless investigations of the fallacious assumption that they had committed sexual indiscretions with white women. This brave female activist, whose life was analytically presented in Alfreda Duster's 1970 edited work entitled *Crusade for Justice: The Autobiography of Ida B. Wells*,[3] demonstrated that her struggle and that of the Africana community was one and the same. Hence, when her male friend Thomas Moss and his business partners, Calvin McDowell and William Stewart, were lynched in Memphis, Tennessee, after opening up a grocery store in a black neighborhood, thereby becoming competitors of the white grocery store owner, she sought to investigate the lynchings of black men in general. She subsequently discovered that most of them were lynched for reasons other than the myth that they had committed America's greatest taboo. Thus, Wells and the countless other female activists collectively represent true, authentic Africana life, one in which race issues and family-centeredness are primary to individualism. According to Sofola, "The world view of the African is rooted in the philosophy of holistic harmony and communalism rather than in the individualistic isolationism of Europe. The principle of relatedness is the *san qua non* of African social reality"(quoted in *Africana Womanism* 58).

Clearly, the Africana woman must insist upon continuing the powerful legacy of a collective liberation struggle for Africana people, as the inequality between the black man and woman is inauthentic relative to our true history. Commenting on the inauthenticity of inequality between men and women in the African community, Daphne Ntiri., in her Introduction to *Africana Womanism: Reclaiming Ourselves*, asserts:

> The concept of equality between men and women
> disappeared due to the advent of foreign forces on
> the continent. The historical forces influenced and
> altered traditional gender roles in Africa. Colonialism
> intensified the sexual division of labor and gender
> subordination in the pre-capitalist modes of produc-
> tion. (10-11)

Taiwo Ajai, the first editor of *African Woman*, a magazine for African women, further explicates how gender discrimination, an inauthentic phenomenon for African life, came to be an integral part of African life today. She focuses on the inauthenticity of the educational, business, political, and social systems imposed on Africa as a part of European colonialism. Consequently Africa, in many ways, has tragically duplicated a rather sexist, Westernized social system.

> In traditional African societies there was much less
> scope than now for discrimination between the sexes.
> Since there was no formal education and no complex
> technical and administrative skills to be acquired, there
> was no opportunity for a great gulf between devel-
> oping men and women . . . . I am not suggesting that
> there was always full participation of women on a
> completely equal basis, but neither was there the com-
> pletely subservient role which some of our men would
> like us to accept today. The dependence of women
> was brought to Africa in part, like so many other "ben-
> efits" of Western civilization, by Europeans—the colo-
> nial administrations and the missionaries. When
> education was first introduced, it was initially for boys
> only. This was the case with higher education and jobs
> in government and business. If girls were permitted
> to get on the ladder at all, it was always several rungs
> below their brothers. In all this of course, our colo-
> nial masters were simply reproducing the system they
> had operated in Europe. [Ajai 78]

As the key concept espoused in *Africana Womanism,* the legacy of the
prevalence of strong, proud, family-centered women of African descent
whose first priority, since the encroachment of white domination over
people of African descent, is race empowerment, it is appropriate to cor-
roborate this critical thesis with another key African-centered theorist.
According to Steady in *The Black Woman Cross-Culturally,* "she [the
black woman] is oppressed not simply because of her sex but ostensibly because of her race . . . "(23). In spite of all, race is primary in
our struggle today as it has been in the past.

As Africana women writers occupy a significant space in the venue
of culture bearers, it is appropriate, then, to reference them in documenting Africana women's lives today and yesterday, with a particular
perusal of the authentic quality of true African life before colonialism.
This will enable one to assess the positive influences of traditional
African life of contemporary African people. In the Foreword to
Mariama Bâ's epistolary novel, *So Long a Letter,* the Senegalese author
calls for a return to traditional practices and customs with the sacred

mission of the writer via "striking out at the archaic practices, traditions and customs that are not a real part of our precious cultural heritage. " She particularly examines and attacks the system of polygamy and the education of female children, both of which reflect a Eurocentric, Islamic system of female subordination, systematically introduced to African life via colonialization. While the European educational system has been well established on the African continent, it can be argued that polygamy, on the other hand, predates colonial infiltration. It should be noted, however, that the pervasiveness of this practice, which inherently subjugates women, was practiced earlier among the elite, but emerged as a widespread practice subsequent to the introduction of Islam during the tenth century. As African historian Cheikh Anta Diop documents,

> Monogamy was the rule at the level of the mass of the people, particularly in Africa. In so far as Africa is considered to be the land of polygamy, it is important to emphasize this fact. In sculptural and pictorial representations, the monogamy of the people is proved by the numerous couples depicted. It seems that this was so in all Africa during the late Middle Ages, until the tenth century, which marks the extension of Islam to the native populations, through the Almoravidiaus. Polygamy tended in this way to become general without ever ceasing to be a sign of social rank. [Diop 126]

Therefore, because history points at these refined practices of female subjugation as inauthentic to overall African life, Bâ, in her novel, attacks the systems of polygamy and the Islamic religion, both of which place the women in a rather vulnerable position, rather than the men directly, as they, too, become subject to an alien lifestyle. To be sure, female subjugation in Bâ's novel can be attributed to historical external influences, particularly European colonialism, an intrusive political system, and the Middle East religion of Islam, which, like European Christianity, perceives women as a commodity. The alien systems, indeed, have disrupted authentic African life.

In *Africana Womanism*, Hudson-Weems accesses the importance of family in *So Long a Letter*:

While Ramatoulaye is concerned with herself and her future, it is only as she exists as a part of a family unit. Her children are a very important part of that family unit and they are essential to her existence. "My love for my children sustained me. They were a pillar; I owed them help and affection" (Bâ 53). It is clear that her decisions are due largely to her commitment to her children's well-being. In the process of keeping her family as a complete family unit, albeit a legal reality only, the protagonist somehow sacrifices her own best interests. (100)

One also becomes keenly aware here of yet two other features of the strong Africana culture bearer—mothering and nurturing—Africana womanist characteristics that one comes to appreciate as true jewels of our rich African heritage. Demonstrating her commitment to motherhood when she discovers that her unmarried daughter is pregnant, the protagonist proclaims:

One is a mother in order to understand the inexplicable. One is a mother to lighten the darkness. One is a mother to shield when lightning streaks the night, when thunder shakes the earth, when mud bogs one down. One is a mother to love without beginning or end. I could not abandon her, as pride would have me do. Her life and her future were at stake, and these were powerful considerations, overriding all taboos and assuming greater importance in my heart and in my mind.... One is a mother so as to face the flood. Was I to threaten, in the face of my daughter's shame, her sincere repentance, her pain, her anguish? Was, I? [Bâ 82-83]

Through it all—colonialization, Islamization, and Westernization— these African womanist features have persevered the threat of destruction for Africana people.

Another important Africana writer is Paule Marshall, an American-born Caribbean writer, whose settings and characters dictate this classification. Her most celebrated novel *Praisesong for the Widow* dramatizes the authentic African legacy of defiance in the Ibos' rebellious refusal to surrender their cultural values. This she depicts in one of her characters, Great Aunt Cuney, the protagonist of the great aunt, who is the supreme paradigm of an Africana woman spiritualist. Avey Johnson comes from a people of tremendous strength and pride, a people endowed with the mystical power to transcend human threats to their rich African legacy. The novel recounts the story of the life of "Avey, short for Avatara" Johnson, who undergoes a spiritual journey of recovery from her acquired sterile Westernized lifestyle, returning to her African roots. We are told of the annual visits she makes as a young girl to her Great-Aunt Cuney, who repeats the story of her lbo ancestors' arrival to the New World and their defiant resistance to it via physical and mystical powers:

> It was here [lbo Landing] that they brought 'em. They taken 'em out of the boats right here where we's standing .... And the minute those Ibos was brought on shore they just stopped, my gran' said, and taken a look around. A good long look. Not saying a word. Just studying the place real good. Just taking their time and studying on it. And they seen things that day you and me don't have the power to see. 'Cause those pure-born Africans was peoples my gran' said could see in more ways than one. The kind can tell you bout things happened long before they was born and things to come long after they's dead .... And when they got through sizing up the place real good and seen what was to come, they turned, my gran' said, and looked at the white folks what brought 'em here .... They just turned ... and walked on back down to the edge of the river here.... They just kept walking right on out over the river. Those lbos! Just upped and walked on away not two minutes after getting here! [Marshall 37-39]

Pervasive in this quotation is the African legacy of defiance and resistance, qualities that have enabled African people to survive. It should be noted also that spirituality[4] an ever existing quality of Africana life pre-

dating colonialism, reigns high here as in the Africana world view, for in
African cosmology, there is the co-existence of the physical and spiritual
worlds, a phenomenon in which both realities compliment one another.

As Aunt Cuney closes her story, we witness the protagonist's
momentary disregard for two long-existing aspects of Africana life—
acknowledgment of spirituality and respect for elders.

> "But how come they didn't drown, Aunt
> Cuney?"
> She had been ten—that old!—and had been
> hearing the story for four summers straight before
> she had thought to ask.
> Slowly, standing on the consecrated ground, her
> height almost matching her shadow which the after-
> noon sun had drawn out over the water at their feet,
> her great-aunt hadturned and regarded her in silence
> for the longest time. It was to take Avey years to forget
> the look on the face under the field. hat, the disap-
> pointment and sadness there. If she could have reached
> up that day and snatched her question like a fIy out
> of the air and swallowed it whole, she would have
> done so. And long after she had stopped going to
> Tatem and the old woman was dead, she was to catch
> herself flinching whenever she remembered the voice
> with the quietly dangerous note that had issued finally
> from under the wide hat brim.
> "Did it say Jesus drowned when he went walk-
> ing on the water in that Sunday School book, your
> momma always sends with you?"
> "No, ma'am.".
> "I didn' think so. You got any more questions?"
> She had shaken her head. "No." [Marshall 39-40]

It was evident that Avey, however for a short while, had not accepted
the legacy of African spirituality, one that allows for the acceptance of
her ancestors' power to see into the past and the future and more important, receptivity to the concept of the myth of the flying African, which
the author evokes in her story of the mystical power of the Ibos to walk

the water. As if it was not enough for Avey to question the powers of the ancestors, as recounted by her Great-Aunt Cuney, in much the same manner in which Morrison's *Beloved* suggests the need for "the reader to pass the stories on, to stand, as does Morrison, and bear witness to them" (Samuels and Hudson-Weems 139), the protagonist also did not respect her aunt, at least enough to receive her story without questioning its legitimacy. In both instances, Avey violated her African values of respect. During the course of the novel, however,

> As Avey discovers herself by reviewing her past connection with her African ancestry via Aunt Cuney, whose dream visitation forces Avey to embark on her quest for the recovery of her lost legacy, she becomes both whole and authentic. Through her aunt's persistence, both verbal and physical, Avey is compelled to recollect her past, her "primal self-nurtured by Great-Aunt Cuney" (Sandiforth 381), and thus, the essence of the Africana womanist takes form. [Hudson-Weems, *Africana Womanism* 115]

In conclusion, therefore, as one examines the traditions, customs, attitudes, and practices of strong, positive women in Africa and in the African diaspora today as model culture bearers, it becomes evident that many of the qualities they possess reflect African culture, thereby establishing the fact that an African continuum is unquestionably in operation. As many of these beliefs and values have been handed down through generations by Africana women in much the same manner as our African historians (griots), thereby establishing them as incredibly strong culture bearers and beacons of a hopeful future, it becomes an authenticating act that many may respect in life and one to which still others may aspire in time. To be sure,

> As white men have focused on keeping Black men in their "place," not allowing them to take care of their families or protect the most precious parts of them (their women and their children), Black women have had to be strong and resourceful in untold ways. [Madhubuti 84]

Hence, to all authentic, strong Africana women bearing our rich family-centered legacy of race empowerment: Pass it on! Pass it on! Pass it on!

Chapter V

Genuine Sisterhood—or Lack Thereof

"Sula?" she whispered, gazing at the tops of trees.
"Sula?"

Leaves stirred, mud shifted; there was the smell
of overripe green things. A soft ball of fur broke and
scattered like dandelion spores in the breeze.

"All that time, all that time, I thought I was missing Jude." And the loss pressed down on her chest
and came up into her throat. "We was girls together,"
she said as though explaining something. "O Lord,
Sula," she cried, "girl, girl, girlgirlgirl."

It was a fine cry—loud and long—but it had no
bottom and it had no top, just circles and circles of
sorrow. [Morrison, *Sula*, 149]

In this poignant closing pronouncement by speaker, Nel Wright, at
the grave site of her alter ego, Sula Peace, some twenty-five years after
her death, Toni Morrison makes a profound comment on the complexity and value of a forever lost friendship between the two women
in *Sula* (149). As the author has proclaimed, she wanted to write about
a profound friendship between two women, and in spite of the complexity of that relationship, which ostensibly appears to be problematic, particularly since Sula has a sexual encounter with her best friend's
husband, Jude, the sum total of their experiences since their childhood
could be expressed as a metaphor for true genuine sisterhood.

Genuine sisterhood, which could be a catalyst by which other

Africana womanist qualities might be advanced to a higher lever, is one of the eighteen characteristics of Africana Womanism as defined by Hudson-Weems in *Africana Womanism*. It is one of the key components for human survival, for the security and harmony of women undergird the strength and structure of society and all its participants. In other words, women are the very foundation of life, whether they know it or not, and thus, they have to be a positive force in life for the ultimate survival of us all. Thus, as the late Sofola asserts "The female gender is the center of life, the magnet that holds the social cosmos intact and alive. Destroy her and you destroy life itself" (*Africana Womanism* xviii). By extension, when we destroy each other, we also destroy humanity since we are, in fact, the backbone of humanity.

Much debate has taken place on the issue of sisterhood, which has been defined as

> a reciprocal [bond] . . . in which each gives and receives equally. In this community of women, all reach out in support of each other, demonstrating a tremendous sense of responsibility for each other by looking out for one another. They are joined emotionally, as they embody empathic understanding of each other's shared experiences. Everything is given out of love, criticism included, and in the end, the sharing of the common and individual experiences and ideas yields rewards. . . . This particular kind of sisterhood refers specifically to an asexual relationship between women who confide in each other and [who] willingly share their true feelings—their fears, their hopes, and their dreams. [Hudson-Weems 65]

The critical need for genuine sisterhood, which is essential for a positive society, cannot be over emphasized, for it is important for women, the family nucleus, to be able to communicate and assist each other in everyday decisions and activities. It is always advantageous to have someone to talk to, someone who is concerned about your needs, someone to give and receive positive feedback and action, both on a personal and a professional basis. As one writer notes, "Black women have a long and colorful tradition of gathering together. Black women are coming together in search of the kind of nurturing, caring and supportive talk that often only another black woman can provide" (Villarosa 82). Given the triple role that the Africana womanist must play—mother, partner and breadwinner—it is very difficult to separate her personal and professional worlds; thus, she needs that support system. To be sure, when one area is neglected, the other suffers as well; when one area soars, the other soars as well. In short, coming from a family-centered reality, the Africana womanist cannot effectively divorce herself from her family, as her job/career is not only important to her but to her family as well. That is to say, both her worlds usually rise or fall together. Significantly, it is often her female support system, or lack thereof, rendering or denying psychological and physical assistance, that either helps or hinders in bringing her immediate or life goals to fruition. According to Patricia Reid-Merritt, who discusses the success of black women via female bounding, "with others they [sisters] engage in kitchen table dialogue, wrap themselves in oral tradition, reinforce cultural nuances, and share personal intimacies" *Sister Power: How Phenomenal Black Women Are Rising to the Top* (178). Hence, where there is a coming together of body, mind, and spirit, there is victory, and Africana women in today's society have much to overcome, given that they are, indeed, victims of a three-fold form of oppression—racism, classism, and sexism.

Another excellent literary example of sisterhood is demonstrated Bâ's short epistolary novel *So Long A Letter*, in which the protagonist, Ramatoulaye, embodies many characteristics of the true Africana womanist, the most obvious ones being genuine in sisterhood, and in family-centeredness. Beginning with the epistolary form of the work itself, its shape takes the form of letter writing between two women, and thereby displaying a strong and reliable friendship, demonstrating a genuineness in sisterhood. Within the friendship the protagonist finds a strong support system that enables her to withstand adversity. The very structure of the novel commands a bond of trust between writer and receiver, which we witness in operation between the protagonist Ramatoulaye and her confidante Aissatou (Hudson-Weems 96-97).

This eighty-five-page letter represents the ultimate in genuine sisterly solidarity:

The kind of friendship these women have goes beyond

confiding in one another and sharing commonalities.
Not only do they share their feelings, they share material things as well. . . . But there is more. Beyond the
sharing is the total empathy that genuine sisterhood
brings. While many are able to sympathize with the
suffering of others, very few are able to truly empathize
with another's pain. [Hudson-Weems 97-98]

The quotation below from the novel itself, demonstrates the level of
profound, lasting friendship the two women share, as Ramotoulaye
recounts the support she receives from her best friend after her husband, Modou, deserts her and their children for Bientou, a classmate
and friend of one of their teenage daughters:

"I shall never forget your response, you, my sister,
nor my joy and my surprise when I was called to the
Fiat agency and was told to choose a car which you
had paid for, in full. My children gave cries of joy
when they learned of the approaching end of their
tribulations, which remain the daily lot of a good
many other students.
Friendship has splendors that love knows not. It
grows stronger when crossed, whereas obstacles kill
love. Friendship resists time, which wearies and severs
couples. It has heights unknown to love.
You, the goldsmith's daughter, gave me your help
while depriving yourself.
Your disappointment was mine, as my rejection
was yours. Forgive me once again if I have re-opened
your wound. Mine continues to bleed." [Bâ 53-55]

Indeed, this is the supreme paradigm of genuine sisterhood, which we
need and would like to see again and again, particularly given the mag-
nitude of stress that Africana women experience daily in a hostile, racist,
white male-dominated society. We need to come together and share
experiences in order to endure and to withstand the everyday suffer-
ings that life holds. Such a friendship as shared by Ramatoulaye and
Aissatou "enables the women to put life into proper perspective and

establish order in their lives" (Hudson-Weems 98). It enables sisters to regroup and to refuel so that they can reemerge as positive strong Africana women, continuing the legacy of togetherness and respect for one another.

Another model example of strong sisterly bonding is the ideal sisterhood between the title character of Gloria Naylor's *Mama Day* and her blood sister, Abigail, of Willow Springs. These elderly elderly sisters consult each other on all matters of importance. They talked to each other before making decisions even in seemingly unimportant matters. In fact, Miranda alias "Mama Day" greets her sister each morning, affectionately referring to her as "sister," and in every way that sacred title was respected. Yet another literary example of strong sisterhood is presented in Zora Neale Hurston's signature novel *Their Eyes Were Watching God*, in which the protagonist, Janie Mae Crawford, and her best friend and confident, Phoebe Watson, engage is an extraordinary sisterly relationship. In fact, it is Phoebe to whom Janie relates her complete heart wrenching continuous love story of her woes and joys with two male chauvinist husbands, "before she finally discovers 'Mr. Right" [Vergible "Tea Cake" Woods], the one man who can respect her as his equal" (Hudson-Weems 79). She trusts her empirically, giving Phoebe the option to tell or to protect her story, which ever she feels is best: "You can tell'em what Ah say if you wants to. Dat's just de same as me 'cause mah tongue is in mah friend's mouf" (Hurston 6). Countering this sisterly bond as the polar opposite, is the situation in which the women in the community do not demonstrate love for one another, particularly toward Janie. They express their inability to treat Janie kindly because Janie's beauty reminds them of what they lack. Although it is evident that women do, in fact, need female bonding in order to give them the strength to continue, most often they do not truly relate to each other in the desired sisterly manner. In our modern-day society, women claim sisterhood as if it is a commonplace phenomenon, knowing full well that the term "sister" is too frequently used lightly or superficially, often without real commitment or sincerity. In other words, contrary to the use of the term in the early sixties and seventies, when women did in fact relate to each other in a more sisterly manner, the term itself has become more of a fashionable rather than a genuine utterance. One need only listen to the national popular dialogue on black women as phenomenon "sisters" and note the publications on the subject to concur that the idea of sisterhood has been too generalized, popularized, and sensationalized as one of the most in vogue colloquialisms today. To be sure, no matter the age, the race, or the class level, today's women treat each other in ways that insult the true idea of sisterhood, as the desired "bonds are often broken or slackened by competitiveness, betrayal, and physical or socioeconomic separation" (Andrews 1). Thus, they gossip about, conspire against, and even callously exclude each other by alienation, one of the most dreaded forms of emotional abuse. Consequently, many women shrink into themselves with an unimaginable sense of paranoia and insecurity, ultimately resulting in not only a distrust of women in particular, but more important, a distrust of humankind in general.

Although we would all like to see more sisterhood among women, this ideal unfortunately is not the norm. In order to achieve this goal, however, we must first candidly analyze the facts. The main culprit in female betrayal is disrespect, under which fall most of the Seven Deadly Sins (pride, avarice, wrath, envy, sloth, gluttony, and lechery). We disrespect and disregard each other's personhood with the individualistic notion that the most important thing in life is self. Moreover, our inflated egos frequently hinder us in extending ourselves to others, particularly in times of need. Thus, as Morrison confesses in her powerful commencement address, delivered at Barnard College in the 1980s,

> I am alarmed by the violence that women do to each
> other: professional violence, competitive violence,
> emotional violence. I am alarmed by the willingness
> of women to enslave other women. I am alarmed by
> a growing absence of decency on the killing floor of
> professional women's worlds. ("Cinderella's Stepsisters"
> 283)

What better way to express the urgent and crucial need for sisterhood in our competitive world of envy and incivility toward each other than in Morrison's indictment offered here. Commenting on her amazement at the cruel manner that women treat each other every day, particularly in the workplace, she offers profound insights into the true nature and source of the absence of sisterhood on the part of many women towards each other, an unfortunate phenomenon that violates the very foundation of female relationships. Moreover, in our pride and self-centeredness, we disallow ourselves a sense of humility that would enable us to apologize, particularly when we have miserably wronged each another. Refusal to apologize when warranted could conceivably result in the loss of a potentially life-long friendship simply because of over weaning pride.

Another human frailty, greed, results in placing too much emphasis on material gains. For example, we go to any lengths to accumulate wealth, including selfishly hoarding resources. In so doing, we refuse to share and network among ourselves, fearing that others could possibly benefit while lessening our own individual gains. Moreover, we often avoid helping each other because too many of those on top condescend and shun those on the bottom rather than reach back to bring those less fortunate sisters forward for the ultimate improvement of all. In confronting this problem, Morrison offers the following:

> I am suggesting that we pay as much attention to our nurturing sensibilities as to our ambition. We are moving in the direction of freedom, and the function of freedom is to free somebody else. You are moving toward self-fulfillment, and the consequences of that fulfillment should be to discover that there is something just as important as you are and that just-as-important thing may be Cinderella—or your stepsister. [283]

Never has this sin been more prevalent than it is today in the competitive world of the workplace, where base betrayal and socioeconomic separation take place. And never has it been more urgent than now to correct this flaw in ourselves if we expect to move forward positively in this new millennium.

Sometimes out of sheer animosity, we gossip and denigrate each other. Out of personal resentment and frustration with ourselves, and the world, we bitterly say cruel things about our sisters. Oftentimes this is because of petty jealousy that we complain of not liking a particular sister simply because of the way that she looks, talks, or presents herself. Remember, it is Shakespeare's Othello, whom Iago ironically warns— "Beware . . . the green-ey'd monster which doth mock/the meat it feeds on" (*Othello* 3.3.165-67). Out of professional envy, we begrudge each other's successes or cannot bring ourselves to acknowledge the other's accomplishments with simple congratulations, believing that somehow giving a fellow sister recognition would somehow diminish our own importance. It may very well be that the heart of the matter is low self-esteem or lack of self-confidence, deficiencies—the tendency to diminish another who may vulnerably stand as yet another victim of individual malice—that could be corrected and hopefully ended forever.

Morrison, reflecting on the many disservices by women against women daily, both inside and outside the workplace, offers possible solutions to this problem, while demanding that evil towards fellow sisters cease:

> I want not to ask you but to tell you not to partici-
> pate in the oppression of your sisters. Mothers who
> abuse their children are women, and another woman,
> not an agency, has to be willing to stay their hands.
> Mothers who set fire to school buses are women, and
> another woman, not an agency, has to tell them to
> stay their hands. Women who stop the promotion of
> other women in careers are women, and another
> woman must come to the victim's aid. Social and wel-
> fare workers who humiliate their clients may be
> women, and other women colleagues have to deflect
> their anger. [283]

Here she urges women to embrace each other with love and concern, rather than oppress each other out of confusion, jealousy, or anger. She comments on the fact that all too often we, as a part of the community of women, relate negatively to each other, which consequentially results in our missing out on the many good things that life has to offer. It is true that if we but reach out to each other, the world would be a much better place to live. Everyone would come out the winner, for in doing good, good, in turn, would inevitably come back to you. In this sense, we would experience karma, as postulated in Hindu philosophy, which is the relation between cause and effect, or in the case of individual ethical behavior, the governing factors for those relations. Hence, karma represents your getting back whatever is put forth, be it good or bad. In this same way, the Bible speaks of reaping what you sow.

This idea could be extended to the specificity of women and their interaction with each other; therefore women should create for themselves, and for their fellow sisters and humankind alike, all the joys that life might possibly hold and in return offer them. We, as sisters, must shield ourselves, and each other from many of life's misfortunes, many of which stem from various forms of abuse, betrayal, and alienation. If one were to really consider the phenomenon of female self-inflicted victimization, one might agree that we are, indeed, responsible for both ourselves, and each other, for both our fortunes and our misfortunes. In assuming that responsibility, we might ultimately end victoriously, as it might result in making possible the most significant victory that we, as individuals or as a collective, could hope to realize—the fruition of ultimate joy.

When something goes wrong, the first step toward correcting it is admitting that the problem exists. Hence, perception must meet reality. Too frequently we are in denial about situations and relationships in our lives that need repair. For example, in feigning naivete or lack of knowledge regarding the scarcity of genuine sisterhood, we are, in fact, denying the existence of unsisterly behavior. This often occurs when we either pretend that something exists that doesn't or when we focus more on the ideal, rather than expose adversarial behavior in hopes of eradicating it. Calling attention to the destructive, self destructive, and inauthentic behavior might very well command its demise. Given that we know all too well how comforting sisterhood is, we must welcome it and its rewards for others as well as for ourselves. Thus, for the moment, let us reflect on how much more beautiful our world would be if all sisters simply loved each another. Our children would be more secure, for they would have not just one female guardian, but many to attend to their everyday needs. As the ancient African proverb goes, "It takes a village to raise a child," a truism that former First Lady Hillary Rodham Clinton observed in her much celebrated and frequently quoted 1996 title, *It Takes a Village*, which remained on the Best Sellers list for twenty weeks that year. As for our men, they, too, would be better partners in our male-female relationships, understanding now the true power of sisterhood and, more important, understanding and acknowledging the role that they themselves play in bringing about and perpetuating unsisterly conduct. Once women "get themselves together," their male counterparts would have little choice but to follow. For example, women

could no longer be pitted against each other. Both physically and emotionally abusive male-female relationships would decline significantly,
with the realization that women are now in support of each other rather
than in opposition. Their support of each other would aid in uplifting
their self-esteem, indeed, a necessary ingredient in their refusal to be
physically and/or emotionally disrespected by their male companions.
With this needed support system in place, women would be better able
to rise up against all forms of abuse related to incidences of the bat-
tered female by her male counterpart. In the end, men would truly
learn to respect the institution and constitution of womanhood and
sisterhood, as they would respect our refusal to compete for their companionship while sacrificing our true selves and/or betraying sisterly
love. Since many solid female relationships are broken when competition and betrayal (e.g, physical attraction to the male counterpart and/or
adultery) move in, we would witness a shift in this phenomenon as our
attitudes towards each other shift. If we but forestall such temptations,
the world would be a better place for all humankind; all would be able
to embrace and enjoy true respect, self-esteem, love, and happiness.
Sisterhood, indeed, undergirds the Africana family, thereby establishing
our collective role in society.

What we obviously fail to understand is that we are participating
in a vicious cycle of misery and doom, for one cannot expect love and
happiness without first offering those things to the universe. When I
speak in terms of the universe, I am speaking of substantive things, for
instance an individual occupying positive space. Why not share that
warm experience with another sister? Here again Morrison says it well:

> In your rainbow journey toward the realization of per-
> sonal goals, don't make choices based only on your
> security and your safety. Nothing is safe.... But in pur-
> suing your highest ambitions, don't let your personal
> safety diminish the safety of your stepsister. In wield-
> ing the power that is deservedly yours, don't permit it
> to enslave your stepsisters. Let your might and your
> power emanate from that place in you that is nurtur-
> ing and caring." ["Cinderella's Stepsisters," 83-4]

Further, to paraphrase the old saying, we are our sisters' keepers. Let me, then, suggest that we take one simple but giant step in reversing this vicious and self-destructive cycle. Whenever you find yourself emitting negative rather than positive energy, you must stop and ask yourself one question. Does this benefit me or anyone else for that matter? Better still, would it not be better to play a positive role, helping someone realize happiness rather than contributing to that person's grief? If, for no reason other than just doing it for yourself, remember that the world does operate on an echo system. What you put out inevitably comes back and returns twofold, threefold, or even more in other ways. Would it not then be better for you to receive multiple successes and blessings rather than multiply failures and misfortunes? The question is rhetorical, of course. Unless you are self-destructive, you would most likely prefer, justifiably so, to join the community of complete, well-rounded, loving sisters, as described in Mona Lake Jones' colorful poem, "A Room Full of Sisters":

A room full of sisters, like jewels in a crown
Vanilla, cinnamon, and dark chocolate brown . . .

Now picture yourself in the midst of this glory
As I describe the sisters who were part of this story.

They were wearing purple, royal blues and all shades of reds
Some had elegant hats on their heads.

With sparkling eyes and shiny lips
They moved through the room swaying their hips.
Speaking with smiles on their African faces
Their joy and laughter filled all the spaces.

They were fashionable and stylish in what they were wearing
Kind sisters who were loving and caring.

You see, it's not about how these sisters appeared
Their beauty was in the value they revered.

They were smart, articulate and well read
With all kinds of Black history stored in their heads.

Jugglers of profession, managers of lives
Mothers of children, lovers and wives.

Good-hearten reaching out to others
Giving back to the community and supporting our brothers.

All of these sisters struggled the past
Suffered from prejudice, endured the wrath.

But they brushed off their dresses and pushed on the door
And they came back stronger than they were before.

Now, imagine if you will
The essence and thrill

As you stand feeling proud
In the heart of this crowd

Sisterhood of modern Sojourners today
Still out in front blazing the way.

A room full of sisters, like jewels in a crown
Vanilla, cinnamon, and dark chocolate brown.

(From *The Color of Culture*)

To be sure, this poem, which presents a dramatic commentary on the beauty of genuine sisterhood, explores the richness, the power, and the pure pleasure of a rare and wholesome bonding among sisters. It anticipates the joy of reciprocal sisterly acts, while making possible the common reality of sisterhood. It is a relationship that allows participants to share their sacred and innermost thoughts, to confide in each other, and in so doing, lay bare one's most intimate and often times joyous experiences. Thus, each gives and receives mutual support in standing up on behalf of the other and, by extension on behalf of our entire Africana community. Such is the way it must be among Africana women if true success, peace, and harmony are to reign.

Chapter VI

Africana Male-Female Relationships and Sexism in the Africana Community

I remain persuaded of the inevitable and necessary complementarity of man and woman.

Love, imperfect as it may be in its content and expression, remains the natural link between these two beings.

To love one another! If only each partner could move sincerely towards the other! If each could only melt into the other! If each would only accept the other's successes and failures! If each would only praise the other's qualities instead of listing his faults! If each could only correct bad habits without harping on about them! If each could penetrate the other's most secret haunts to forestall failure and be a support while tending to the evils that are repressed!

The success of the family is born of a couple's harmony, as the harmony of multiple instruments creates a pleasant symphony.

The nation is made up of all the families, rich or poor, united or separated, aware or unaware. The success of a nation therefore depends inevitably on the family. (Bâ 88-89)

The above quotation is from the Senegalese novel, *So Long a Letter*, by Mariama Bâ. The protagonist, Ramatoulaye, offers excellent pointers concerning love and marriage. In her reflections on her marriage, the advice she gives represents the ideal in male-female relationships, which unfortunately she was unable to experience, not necessarily because of any identifiable faults of her own, but rather because of the decisions her husband Modou makes about marriage and commitment, based, for the most part, upon the external forces and practices of legalized polygamy in the Islamic communities of Senegal. Thus, Ramatoulaye contends that, in her country, "all women have almost the same fate, which religions or unjust legislation have sealed" (88).

Shifting from the continent of Africa to America, the subject of Africana male-female relationships remains a much-discussed issue. Attempts to reassess these relationships command an engagement in historicizing circumstances of Africana people, which includes not only focusing on the matter of the personal love between a couple, but also considering the impact of the social, political, economic, and cultural milieu on the total Africana family as well. The following quotation comments on the history of Africana male-female relationships in America based upon a support system in the face of racial adversity, an Africana womanist priority that has been replaced today with women's issues, many of them, unfortunately by Black women:

> Until the 1950s, strong relationships existed between black women and black men. They were the major factor in keeping racism from destroying the black family and the black community in America. Now, it has been replaced, in many instances, by a war between genders—a war in which there can be no winners..The real casualties will be the black families and black children of America. [Reynolds, xi]

The searing fifties and sixties ushered in two significant, politicized phenomena: The first was the advent of the inception of the modern civil rights movement ignited by the brutal lynching of Emmett Louis "Bobo" Till, a fourteen-year-old Black Chicago youth, for whistling at a twenty-one-year old white woman, Carolyn Bryant, in Money, Mississippi, on 28 August, 1955. This horrific incident occurred just three months and three days prior to Rosa Parks' refusal to relinquish her bus seat to a white man in Montgomery, Alabama, 1 December,

1955. The second, culminating in the sixties, was the rise in popular-
ity of avenues or places for women in society, accurately characterizing
the age of the woman, which brought forth the women's liberation
movement, led by Betty Friedan, one of the shapers of modern day
feminism, and the author of *The Feminist Mystique*. With this new emphasis on women and gender issues came increased de-emphasis of the
black liberation struggle. This new wave of feminism had a decidedly
negative impact on the Africana community, particularly on the Africana
family with regard to its male-female relationships, the very foundation of positive Africana life. But that is not the only threatening force
in the black community. Sexism, too, plays its part in dividing our community, as this menacing factor wreaks havoc on the sanctity and harmony of the Africana family. Thus, with the weight of racial oppression
and diabolical pressures still omnipresent since the involuntary migra-
tion and arrival of Africans to this continent, along with the patriarchal
system of sexism and female subjugation, strained relations between
Africana men and women have become a salient phenomenon in the
Africana community.

For centuries, Africana men and women have been forging a collective battle against racist oppression in America. This two-prong support system, the male-female collective struggle, which is one of the
eighteen descriptors for Africana womanism, has proven to be the
most effective in combating racism. Africana womanism, which insists
upon this mutual respect and inclusivity, strives to break the gender
barriers between the Africana man and woman. It becomes clear, then,
that while the most devastating threat to our community remains
racism, some serious attention must also be given to Africana male-
female relationships, wherein lies the survival of the Africana family and,
by extension, the entire Africana community. To be sure, strong bonds
between Africana couples must be established in order that the black
liberation struggle be strengthened and therefore empowered.
According to black arts poet and critic Haki R. Madhubuti, who takes
the political stance of the interlocutory nature of black male-female relationships and the on-going black liberation struggle:

> Black couples must understand that "Black love" in the
> United States is much more than a commitment
> between two people; it is also the realization that there

are political, economic, historical, racial, familial, and emotional forces impacting upon that loveship. [Madhubuti, 180]

Further, he asserts:

The root as well as the quality of Black life is in the relationship established between Black men and women in a white supremacist system. Black struggle, that is, the liberation of our people, starts in the home. [Madhubuti 60]

Given such contentions by one of our most unrelenting black culturalist and liberation advocates since the sixties, a period that has been historically characterized as an all-time high point of the black liberation struggle, it becomes critical that the personal relationship between the Africana couple be perfected if the family unit constituting the over-all Africana community is to survive. Moreover, Madhubuti's assessment here accurately identifies the controlling ingredients necessary for a long-lasting, positive Africana male-female relationship, one that includes not only emotional and physical components, but historical, political, and economical dynamics as well. Necessarily, the Africana male-female relationship requires a unified commitment from both parties, a commitment they share for the benefit of their personal and communal fulfillment. The focus on the complexity of the Africana community, then, emulating from the love between Africana men and women, sets forth the parameters for analyzing the dynamics of Africana male-female relationships and for establishing plausible strategies to make them work.

Because many Africana women have shifted their allegiance from the struggle against racial oppression to the struggle against gender oppression in the midst of the women's era, Africana men have begun to feel alienated, believing that their female counterparts are abandoning them and the liberation struggle, a belief that, no doubt has some merit. Understanding that the primary concern for the feminist is female empowerment rather than race empowerment, their feelings of betrayal, frustration, abandonment, and the likes are natural. Some may even call it paranoia on the part of the Africana man;

but whatever one calls it, it exists. Sociologist Dolores Aldridge comments on this element of betrayal in *Focusing: Black Male-Female Relationships* (35). With this in mind, it must be noted that in the final analysis, when those Africana women finish fighting the feminist battle and feminists have succeeded in realizing all their goals relative to female empowerment, the Africana woman will be left with the reality that she is both black and at the bottom. Such was the case with the June 1995 Supreme Court ruling on the unconstitutionality of Affirmative Action Set Asides that were racially based. Those based on gender equality were found constitutionally sound but the black woman remains classified as black first. Hence, the Africana woman, after a lengthy absence from the black liberation struggle, will then find herself coming back to her male counterpart and to her community to pick up the on going liberation struggle for her entire family.

The threat of the female-centered, female-empowerment ideology of feminism undoubtedly has begun to diminish the significance of the traditional family-centered, race-empowerment philosophy of the black liberation movement. Refocusing this political orientation of the Africana woman, in conjunction with her family, has resulted in weakening the Africana community. In Contrast, operating within the constructs of an Africana womanist paradigm, then, reshifts the focus away from race myopic feminism to African-centered solutions to the breakdown in Africana male-female relationships. Such solutions are grounded in three key interconnecting components—the centrality of family, the love for each other, and the commitment to the liberation struggle for ultimate survival. Needless to say, viewing the problems through the paradigm of Africana womanism in order to bring about total parity for Africana men and women in a racist society must establish identify the critical issues impeding their progress.

Africana womanism, necessarily must first contend with the disharmony within the Africana family, that pervades and penetrates all aspects of the lives of Africana men and women, especially their personal/love relationships. Disharmony, which is frequently the result of financial hardships, lack of commitment to each other and to the overall Africana community, and the lack of trust and communication, are inextricably linked to our emotional strife. What this suggests, then, is that rather than taking an oppositional posture in reaction to perceived unresolvable differences between men and women,

Africana womanism instead highlights a structure wherein Africana women work with Africana men in dissolving both the sense of alienation that Africana men experience and the sense of isolation and suppression that Africana women experience.

In the case of the Africana male, participation in all aspects of the culture is encouraged. For example, he, as is the case of the woman, is charged with the responsibilities of accepting his shortcomings/limitations and acknowledging them in a sharing attempt to redirect the outcome. Expounding on this reciprocal nature of positive male-female relationships, Madhubuti asserts that The African American man must always listen to his partner, the black man must also be able to reciprocate. He must involve himself in all aspects of housework. He must involve himself in the birth of his children. He must always accept the blame for his own imperfections and try to change for the better (181-183). With these mandates for positive relationships come genuine caring and compassion, both of which foster a positive dependency of one upon the other. It should be noted here that needing one another is not a negative practice; thus, there is no need to apologize for needing each other's love and presence. Only when one can admit to and appreciate this interdependency can a relationship truly grow into something beautiful and permanent. As stated in *Africana Womanism*,

> Positive male companionship is of great interest to the Africana womanist in general, for she realizes that male and female relationships are not only comforting but the key to perpetuating the human race. Without each other, the human race becomes extinct. The Africana womanist also realizes that, while she loves and respects herself and is, in general, at peace with herself, she ultimately desires a special somebody to fill a void in her life, one who makes her complete. [Hudson-Weems 67]

Na'im Akbar expounded on this concept in his 1989 contribution "Materialism and Chauvinism," wherein he concludes:

> African American men and women must not fall

victim to the expanding unisexualism so prevalent in American society. They must preserve the uniqueness of their separate, complementary roles. They must also avoid ontological weakness which equates nurturance, dependence, dependence and supportiveness with weakness. They must also avoid the highly destructive macho notions of manhood which are feverishly trying to be realized by both men and women in their striving for a faulty liberation (55).

Clearly, a realization of Africana womanist goals for a harmonious Africana male-female relationship demands reincorporation of the Africana male from his position of alienation from his family and community to a cooperative center with the strength of his female counterpart. It is equally important that each partner have realistic expectations in a relationship rather than unrealistic demands , that may only end in disappointments, thereby ultimately destroying an otherwise healthy relationship. For example, idealistically women often desire tall, clean cut, educated men with high income. They want it all. Many men, too, though many are often intimidated by their success, want it all, preferring women who are both beautiful and successful. The truth of the matter is that both should be focusing on what each could contribute to a healthy relationship, rather than on selfish needs.

In this respect, there is little room, if any, for selfishness. The goal, then, becomes what is good for the whole, i.e. for the family, rather than what is in it for the self. Of course, there are problems of financial support and the lack of sufficient, not excessive, funds, which often result, in some instances, in a lack of mutual respect and even in low self-esteem. However, if the relationship has more fun and lightheartedness, that is, laughter that the joy of true friendship can create, it is easier to cope with financial shortcomings. Indeed, if there is no relief, there is little hope for a relationship laden with boredom, complaints, and unrelenting gravity, compounded by the problem of limited funds. Not surprisingly, what we witness with the Africana man, much like the Africana woman, is his heretofore unacknowledged tripartite plight— race, class, and gender; that is, long-standing traditional male roles dictated by a white, racist, patriarchal system, that makes unrealistic demands on Africana men, who have historically been disenfranchised.

> Africana men, too, [like the Africana woman] have
> not had the consistent experience of upholding the
> traditional role of the male as the head of the house-
> hold. In a traditional patriarchal system the male is
> expected to fulfill the responsibilities outside the
> home, such as earning money, while serving as the
> official head inside the home. On the home base, he
> dictates the order of the household and designates
> the woman to carry it out. [Hudson-Weems 64]

This particularly contentious issue within Africana families with the
male as breadwinner is particularly problematic, as his lack of resources
has often rendered him impotent in earning sufficient wages to defray
household expenses without the assistance of his female counterpart.
In fact, the often-touted two-family income, a marker of progressive
modern evolution of the family structure, is in reality a necessity for the
Africana family. Paradoxically, in the society we live in, it is also an indi-
cator of the inferior status of the Africana male and the devolution of the
Africana family structure. Given this heavy gender burden based upon
a class system in which capital is unequally distributed, the economic
predicament of the Africana male represents one of the most complex
dilemmas facing Africana male-female relationships. Nathan Hare, in
Crisis in Black Sexual Politics suggests a positive response to the financial
predicament of Africana men and women in the following quotation:

> The young Black woman will do well to be sup-
> portive of her man while remaining firm in her rights,
> understanding while not necessarily condoning her
> mate's hesitation in the face of unfair adversity. Rather
> than chastise her man, however, for his mediocre
> occupation, she might better find something good to
> say while remaining alert to signs of simmering ambi-
> tion on his part as a basis for further encouragement
> on hers. [125]

Such a situation breeds another monster—drug or alcohol abuse, ultimately erupting into domestic violence as a means of escape and pressure release. This harsh scenario is exemplified in the underlying theme of Terry McMillan's *Disappearing Acts*: The Africana man is trapped within a patriarchal model and its attendant abuses. This narrative of the almost insurmountable challenges and the unconquerable spirit of black love, is demonstrated in the frustrating predicament of the two protagonists, Zora and Franklin. Though ultimately they overcome such potentially debilitating and life-threatening illnesses as drug and alcohol abuse and epilepsy, this Africana couple provides an encouraging model. They draw attention to the need for Africanan people to successfully navigate through communal and professional resources for healing and recovering from our physical and emotional illnesses. Hence, there is no way to have a wholesome relationship if one is not in control of one's faculties, which have been altered by the intrusion of alien agencies. Such control can be neither recovered nor maintained in a state of "selfish" individualism. That said, it must be added that as literature reflects reality, much truth emerges from fiction. Such is the case of *Disappearing Acts*.

As a novel whose characters are committed to a positive male-female relationship and making it work, *Disappearing Acts* abounds in the Africana womanist characteristic of being in concert with the male counterpart in the struggle. In it, Franklin is the product of the "last hired, first fired syndrome," which is a direct result of racism. In spite of everything, Zora does not consider his inability to maintain employment a reflection of his manhood or of any lack thereof. Although Franklin's pride makes it difficult for him to accept her constant financial support, she sticks by him, even making some personal sacrifices in the process.

> Franklin. Didn't I make you float? Didn't I give you spring in winter? Didn't I show you rainbows and everything else that moved inside me? I gave birth to your child because I loved you. I stuck by you when you were broke, because I loved you. I stuck by you for everything, because I loved you. So tell me, goddammit, wasn't that enough? [McMillan 366]

Of course, this tirade comes after Zora is forced to have Franklin removed from their apartment because of physical violence and its continuing threat. Even so, in doing this, she is, in fact, loving herself and her child enough to grant him the space he needs to recover, which he ultimately does. "It takes a lot for Zora to come to this decision, but she realizes that this is the only way Franklin can save himself and their relationship. He has to redeem himself. She is not able to do it for him, although she has tried to many times before" (Hudson-Weems 140). Fortunately for this family unit, in the end there is hope for them, although this is not always the case in our communities.

Ironically, both the core of declining Africana male and female relationships and its solutions lie predominately in three critical issues: (i) reciprocal appreciation of each other, which Maulana Karenga defines as a "positive sharing and its mutual investment in each other's happiness, well-being and development"; (ii) the politics of economics, as outlined above in the triple plight of Africana men and women; and (iii) the establishment of an authentic value system that promotes a collective liberation struggle which compliments personal relationships. Along these lines, Karenga cites black sociologists Joyce Ladner and Robert Staples, who argue for "the need for a value system which rejects and counters the standards of the dominant society" (Karenga 295). This is the very " value system" manifested in the paradigmatic structure of Africana womanism, for too many Africanans have brought European cultural values and perspectives to their relationships. According to Belle, Bouie, and Baldwin:

> African Americans continue to negotiate their survival in a society where the major institutions are governed by the principles and values of the Euro-American worldview. Having existed in a Eurocentric social reality over several centuries, evidence suggests that African Americans have become psychologically dependent, in varying degrees, on that reality. Consequently, they have accepted an orientation to social relationships, which is more consistent in many respects with Eurocentric cultural definitions than with their own Afrocentric cultural definitions. This state of psychological oppression means that many African American males and females have internalized Eurocentric definitions/values and practice them

in their relationships. [50-51]

Karenga's identification of the four basic connections (cash, flesh, force, and dependency), expounds on problems in Africana male-female relationships that are informed by this inauthentic value system for blacks. In erroneously assuming that money is the solution to all problems, and that, in fact, it buys whatever is desired, including your partner, we find ourselves slipping into a commercial, materialistic mode of thinking, reflective of a value system created by Western culture. To be sure, this is an inauthentic behavior pattern relative to an Africana perspective that needs correcting. This is not to say that we do not need finances to survive; however, extravagance and over abundance are not parts of the real equation for the lives of authentic Africana people. Admittedly, finances play a large part in the security of relationships, and thus, while it is difficult to acknowledge, when finances fall into trouble, relationships, too, fall into trouble. It is evident that a relationship does not exist in a vacuum, and thus, the couple's financial stability invariably affects how they interact on all fronts. When we find ourselves in a financial bind, i.e. when bills cannot be paid, when necessities cannot be met, we subsequently find ourselves in a stressful mode, operating under the stressful circumstances of financial strife and depravation. Unfortunately, this reality is all to often the case with Africana couples who sadly enough are often the victims of racial discrimination.

The "last hired, first fired" scenario has much validity, for as Susan Ferguson so aptly puts it, "when the ax falls, [blacks] usually have even fewer resources than whites to help them through the tough times" (Ferguson 533). This is certainly not to suggest that every circumstance regarding financial hardships is a matter of racism. We cannot, however, deny the frequency of its occurrence either, for its victimization does not stop there. It insinuates itself into every personal corner of one's existence, into our private relationships and intimate places. No matter how hard we fight it, we cannot feign peace and happiness when we are unable to meet everyday necessities that depend upon solvency. We may swoon into infidelity or even find ourselves saying unkind things to each other, with an overwhelming air of impatience and venom, as if our partner is at all times the culprit in this unwelcome and unpleasant situation. Sadly, the saying "no money, no honey," which rings true to some degree, is illustrative of the tremendous breakdown in mutual respect between Africana men and women. Clearly, both partners have to remember that rules governing human relationships are not necessarily applicable to financial ones. Successful male-female relationships operate within a core realm of mutual respect and love for one another. The Africana man must understand and appreciate his female counterpart. He must respect her as mother, culture bearer, and co-partner. To disrespect her is to disrespect self. Likewise, the Africana woman must realize that the Africana man is father, protector, and co-partner. As such, he, too, is deserving of reciprocal love and respect. Simply put, there must be reciprocal love and respect for one another before a lasting wholesome relationship can truly exist.

For Africana people, there is also the element of confusion in prioritizing that leads to a tendency of appropriating someone else's agenda, reflecting someone else's particular priorities. As an African people, we come from a collective and family-centered perspective, with emphasis on the intertwined nature of our destiny as a whole. With that in mind, then, the question of the feminist agenda comes to the forefront as to whether it is taking its toll on today's Africana community. Does it negatively impact upon Africana male-female relationships? Can feminist language and attitudes, which some find problematic largely because of some strong anti-male overtones, work in the home place as well as in the work place for Africana people? And finally, are there options relative to creating positive Africana male-female relationships, the foundation of an ideal family structure, in order to ensure a more holistic life for all? Indeed, these critical questions are at the crux of the matter in instigating the breakdown in positive Africana male-female relationships. Without positive interdependence and interrelationship between the sexes, including the creation of our own authentic language as a means of communicating and defining our authentic activities and existence as an Africana people, positive male-female relationships will not be possible, which translates into the ultimate extinction of Africana families/communities. This is devastation!

As Africana womanism proposes most of eighteen distinct features characterizing the Africana woman, it proposes most of the same features for the male counterpart. Both are self-namers, self-definers, family-centered, in concert with their counterparts in the liberation struggle; flexible role players, strong, ambitious, respectful of elders, whole, and authentic. Additionally, the true Africana man is female compatible, moral, role model, supportive, respectful of women, protective, fathering, and loving. It is important to understand that recognition of and respect for the existence of a higher power, (spirituality/morality) which guides personal and social behavior and thus prohibits immoral acts like infidelity, perversion, etc., are the penultimate qualities of any positive and complete male-female relationship. In other words, without a spiritual presence in our lives, all else is null and void. Moreover, if both men and women aspire to perfecting themselves by adopting these qualities in their lives, they would then find the kind of mutual love, respect, and support that could only lead to an ideal spirit-guided relationship between the two.

It is crucial, then, for Africana men and women to work diligently toward tailoring their own agenda, so that their needs and concerns may be more accurately and expediently addressed. This includes the specific problems of the Africana woman today, particularly as some have unsuccessfully tried to address their needs through a feminist construct or paradigm. In this regard, the lines of common action are blurred, which prohibiting the existence of any true positive black male-female relationship. It is here that the couple can truly open up their hearts, expressing their needs and desires, as well as confessing and admitting their shortcomings and mistakes. "I am sorry," the three magic words that are key to positive male-female relationships, can begin the healing process for a troubled relationship. To be sure, admitting fault usually leads to forgiveness. Such common action and commitment without fear, wherein each partner listens to the other as a means of sharing, ultimately promote the kind of bonding necessary for making positive male-female relationships.

On the subject of commitment, Staples has paralleling theories for both women and men. For the former, he believes that "Some have a fear of making a commitment and suffering the fate of many black women [that is] being rejected and winding up as a divorcee with children to support" (Staples, 78). Such fear generating from women due large in part to their being products of broken homes. Men, Staples contends that "due to the Black man's desire to maintain control of his situation, and his image of masculinity, refusal to make a commitment is one way of achieving the power balance in a relationship" (Staples, 79). Insecurity makes him fear that the woman may dictate the nature of the relationship and take control of its destiny. In avoiding ties, he escapes this dreaded possibility. Of course, all too frequently there is the issue of consciously relegating problem solving to women, which they often do without male input. Moreover, the "excess number of Black women in the eligible pool and the concentration of so many educated, attractive women and their implicit sexual and emotional demands may overwhelm them. With so many women to choose from, it becomes more difficult for Black men to form committed relationships" (Staples 77). Unquestionably, the over abundance of female choices distracts from the need of many Black men to make commitments.

Continuing with the focus on habits prohibiting positive Africana male-female relations, there is the issue of the wide-spread incarceration of Africana men, which is a rapidly growing phenomenon. Many studies examine the racist aspect of the pervasive incriminization process of Africana men. According to one source, "When African-Americans are subjected to trial, they [Africana men] are often given especially harsh sentences" (Miller 76). With this kind of sentencing comes a decline in employment, for criminal records often have a direct connection to unemployment. The problem is indeed mind-boggling. We can only hope that someone will soon introduce a means of truly exposing this unjust practice, thereby breaking this vicious cycle that impacts negatively on the Africana family. Moreover, there is the problem of womanizing, whoring [as in the case of the woman], selfishness, homosexuality, and bisexuality, all of which play a large role in the breakdown in Africana male-female relations. Womanizing and whoring remain critical and legitimate concerns for many men and women today, as many of them desire monogamous relationships for love and/or fear of contacting fatal diseases. In the case of the male, perhaps because of the "male shortage," many men believe they should have "carte blanche" regarding the number of women they should have, with no questions asked. Unfortunately, having several women does not necessarily guarantee true love or happiness, which is why so many men are still of the opinion that it really only takes the right person to make one really and truly happy.

The matter of selfishness is another big problem in Africana male-female relationships. While it is difficult to pinpoint just where this propensity originates, I am of the opinion that women, as culture bearers, mothers and nurturers, three of the eighteen characteristics of Africana Womanism, we are in many ways responsible for rearing these generations of selfish beings, individuals who almost always make their decisions based on what they themselves want or need, rather than on what is most beneficial to the family. In any event, the only recourse for survival of the Africana male-female relationship is to grow up and put an end to selfishness, thereby putting the family first for a change. On a final note, sexism in the Africana community is an issue that we cannot take lightly. The late Audre Lorde, Africana literary critic and poet, makes the following assessment of racism and sexism in the Africana community:

> Black women's literature is full of the pain of frequent assault, not only by racist patriarchy, but also by Black men. Yet the necessity for and history of shared battle have made us, Black women, particularly vulnerable to the false accusation that anti-sexist is anti-Black. Meanwhile, woman hating as a recourse of the powerless is sapping strength from Black communities and our very lives. [Lorde, 356]

The fact remains that while the number one obstacle to success for Africana people is racism, the problem of sexism in our community continues to rear its ugly head, with the full knowledge that this problem is not only inauthentic but, more important, unfeasible since we are, after all, in a collective struggle for the survival of our entire family— men, women, and children. This is not to say that the Africana woman does not desire total equality with her male counterpart. Quite the contrary, for egalitarianism has always been a key factor in the Africana family, and as equal partners, we must insist upon that status. Granted, there are some real indications of female subjugation in the Africana community, a clear case of black man duplicating the white man's tactics, which are rooted in racism. According to Karenga,

> Racism engenders self-hate, self-doubt and pathological fixation on the white paradigm. And sexism encourages artificial personal power over women as a substitute for real social power over one's destiny and daily life. (292)

For the Africana man there is obviously serious confusion about his logic in regard to power. Believing that oppressing women represents power is absurd, for when he goes beyond that point, the he will still be left with a tremendous sense of powerlessness as to how society regards him, an image that is unaltered and unaffected in any positive sense by his mistreatment of his female counterpart. Consequently, this behavior is counterproductive and hence cannot be tolerated; it must be banned from our community forever. Moreover, we need only scratch the surface to conclude that any thinking person can see through that pose and understand that the Africana man has absolutely no institutionalized power to oppress anybody for that matter, and hence, there is no need for the same kind of antagonism between Africana men and women that exists between white men and women. There is only a need for renegotiation and for clarity about the fact that we are indeed equals and equally oppressed by a racist system.

While it is obvious that men generally have more physical prowess than women, their tendency towards verbal and/or physical abuse of their female counterparts should not be interpreted as a birthright. In futilely seeking their manhood in the subjugation of black women, Africana men fail to understand that they and their female counterparts are inextricably bound together as equals. The problem is that they are unaware of the true source of their pain, a relentless torment they find almost impossible to articulate. The result is their expression of internal struggle superficially alleviated by violence not only towards each other, as manifested in gang violence and drug abuse; but towards women in particular, as manifested in female bashing. In spite of their natural inclination to feel a connection with their women, who complete their sense of being, feeling the brunt of the white man's oppression makes them both vulnerable and sensitive, which is nonetheless manifested by a pose of insensitive behavior. Therefore, they find themselves in the peculiar predicament of hurting the very ones who are "in their corner." Rather than seek vindication for their feelings of frustration and inadequacy on their female counterparts, they would be better to hold the true culprit responsible, perhaps the initial but essential step in helping to eradicate sexism in our community. Moreover, because of economic stresses, high unemployment and low wages, minimum education and illiteracy, for example—Africana men have again taken out their frustrations on their women, oftentimes envying the financial achievements that some Africana women have gained. Cyclical in nature, this anger and frustration continues to feed upon itself. In the final analysis, however, muscle flexing can never translate into having true power, and the sooner Africana men realize this, the sooner we can go on about the business of pursuing what Vivian Gordon calls "the partnership struggle with black men [and black women] for the emancipation of their communities" (Gordon 13). To be sure, Africana men need both their women and their communities at the center of their lives in order to become whole and complete, which could ultimately heal the history of abuse and female subjugation. Because the lives and destinies of Africana men and women are so interconnected, their psychics need to be healed together, facilitating proper nurturing for the survival of our communities and our children, our future.

Because a large part of sexist behavior is societal, it is fairly difficult for men in general to avoid being sexist to some degree. This is because of the way we are taught and trained and the roles men and women are assigned in society. Men continue to hold the most powerful positions in society. The Africanan man mimics white society; yet, his racially based limitations complicate his position, thereby constantly challenging his masculinity. As a consequence, the Africana man, feeling that within his home, one of the few places where he can assert his masculine authority without retribution, he can exert his masculinity, his sense of power over his female counterpart. Needless to say, sexism in the black community, which is a contradiction to our historical reality, must be addressed.

Unlike whites, Africana men and women have been equals from the beginning, as we originated from the continent of Africa, an agricultural land where equal sharing of responsibilities and status is mandatory. This is not to suggest that female subjugation does not currently exist in Africa, for it does. While some levels of oppression of women predate the advent of colonialism in Africa, it was not the kind of exploitative oppression we speak of in terms of female subjugation today. Then, men were conscientious and therefore pledge their commitment to the community. Today sexism in the African family represents a form of European structural duplication. The idea of egalitarianism within the Africana family does not suggest that there are no male and female roles, for there are, indeed, defined roles in our society. What must be made clear, of course, is that the roles in the Africana family are necessarily flexible, as is the case of the Africana womanist as flexible role player. Thus, one role is no less important than another. While sexism may not be totally eradicated within the near future, one can make a conscious effort on a daily basis to correct it. Moreover, our community, like the Africana woman, must prioritize our battles so that the most threatening one to our families and to our communities will have first priority in order to ensure black survival. It is clear that we have our own way of looking at things and of putting those things into proper perspective via prioritization. This does not compromise or lessen the seriousness of sexism nor the need for eradicating this phenomenon, which has penetrated our world and violated our personal lives. Thus, in much the same way that we address the triple plight of Africana women from an Africana womanist perspective, i.e., prioritizing race, class, and gender, while dismissing none of the blows to our existence, we must likewise prioritize our attack on all forms of oppression within the Africana community, including the inauthentic and menacing problem of female subjugation. To be sure, the eradication of this obstacle to the over-all well-being of the Africana family and community would, indeed, lift us to a higher level of harmony and collective struggle, which is necessary to carry us into this new millennium successfully.

As is evident, a Eurocentric blueprint for positive Africana male-female relationships is unrealistic, as "Black male-female relationships, which prioritize Eurocentric values seemingly, would be less stable than Black heterosexual relationships with a stronger Afrocentric cultural foundation" (Belle, Bouie, and Baldwin 52). We must understand that we, Africana men and women, are in this together. We need to recognize that we are each other's better half, and that we need each other in order to work through this crisis. We need to understand that, contrary to some beliefs, we are not each other's enemy, and that, at times, when our self-esteem is at its lowest, when racism has dealt a low blow to both our psyche and our pocketbook, we need to reach out to one another, giving all the love and understanding possible in order for us to evolve as positive beings. True, there may be times when we strike out against that which is closest to us in our moments of frustration and despair, but we must redirect that negative energy, transferring it into some positive soul love for each other, realizing that we need each other now as always and even more than ever today. Hence, Africana men and women working together, represents the only way the global African community can be rejuvenated. Only then can our personal lives be somewhat restored to a state of harmony, security, and happiness, thereby enabling us to move positively to a higher level of existence, free of racism, classism, and sexism.

> The person I love will strengthen me by endorsing my assumption of my manhood [womanhood], while the need to earn the admiration or the love of other will erect a value-making superstructure on my whole vision of the world. [Fanon 41]

Summation List of 13 Positive/Negative Elements of Male/Female Relationships

Positive:
1. Love
2. Friendship
3. Trust
4. Fidelity
5. Truth
6. Mutual Respect
7. Support
8. Humility
9. Fun
10. Compassionate
11. Sharing/Caring
12. Complimentary
13. Spiritual

Negative:
1. Contempt
2. Rivalry
3. Distrust
4. Infidelity
5. Deceit
6. Disrespect
7. Neglect
8. Arrogance
9. Mean-Spirited
10. Callous
11. Selfish/Egocentric
12. Critical
13. Non-Spiritual

Chapter VII

Sister Souljah's *No Disrespect*: The Africana Womanist's Dilemma

> Many feel that Africana women fiction writers have a critical mission to accomplish, which is to "tell it like it is." And since literature in general should reflect life, it is important that the literature of Africana womanist writers speak the truth—the whole truth. When the Africana womanist writes about male-female relationships, for example, she must present them in all dimensions. She must explore the dynamics of the relationships, which go far beyond the mere surface interaction between the man and the woman. She must realistically and objectively examine the dominant forces at play, forces that dictate the very nature of the conflicts and the ways they are handled. These forces, in many instances, are deeply rooted in economics, particularly the economic failure of the Africana man.
>
> When one looks at the economic problems within the Africana family, one invariably comes back to the problem and interference of racism, which strongly impacts upon the economic realities of the Africana family and community. (Hudson-Weems, *Africana Womanism* 77)

The above quotation explicates the underlying mission of an authentic Africana womanist literary piece *par example*. A highly appropri-

ate quotation, it establishes two very important elements for literature, truth, and objectivity, which should stand out in any good analysis. This is precisely the case with *Sister Souljah* (1996), an
autobiographical novel in which "Sister Souljah relates her own experiences and those of others around her as she grew up in the projects,
made her way to [the] university and down the road that has shaped
her into a vocal activist on issues of class, race and gender" (Marrengane
72). As this quotation ends with "class, race and gender," key issues in
the novel of Sister Souljah, we see how appropriate the book is for
this volume, since one of the key issues for the concept of Africana
womanism is the prioritization of race, class and gender. Dealing with
the real world and real people, Sister Souljah carefully delivers the full
story of the life experiences of one of the most unforgettable personas
ever presented, the author herself, in serious quests for both her soul
mate and ways of improving life for young Blacks, particularly those
in the urban areas. Unpretentiously, she graphically lays out her life in
full, bare and raw, and "gives painful but honest insight into male-
female relationships through her experiences growing up in a Bronx
housing project and her college years at Rutgers University" (Shahid,
Book Review). In the end, we celebrate with her the victory of becoming a true Africana womanist, one who keeps her priorities and focus
on the survival of the Africana family, men, women, and children as
an instrument by which this goal may be realized. Make no mistake,
at the end of the day, Sister Souljah, through her oddessy culminating
in her becoming an evolved model Africana womanist, ultimately
emerges as one who truly counts in the Africana community, one
who must offer assistance and possible solutions to the plight of Africana
people and the relentless fight for not just mere existence but rather
real survival on every level.

In the very opening of the book, the author establishes the fact
that racism is the most critical issue confronting the Africana family,
its past, its present and its future, which negatively affects our "ability
to relate to and love one another in healthy life-giving relationships"
(Souljah, xiv). According to the author's review of her own book, she
"delineates 'institutionalized unhappiness,' if you will in which families living on the urban plantations of American cities are eerily similar. This condition she diagnoses as a persistent hangover from five-plus
centuries of slavery" (Souljah, *Book Review*). Thus, she asserts she came

to truly "understand how the day-to-day pressures of being black, penniless, structureless, culturally restricted, and frustrated in America could tear away at something that was supposed to be sacred: our loved ones and our family" (41). While Sister Souljah's sense of hopelessness has some merit, it is important to point out that if we observe the powerful African tradition of "Sankofa," which means "looking backward to move forward," and if we are true to our rich legacy of collectivity and familihood, we would accept ultimate responsibility for our lives, in spite of the negative role that others have played and continue to play in our lives. This empowering history would make us even more resolute in our family-centeredness, which would make us more supportive of each other as we forge stronger Africana families. Indeed, these driving forces in our lives, both before and during slavery, have enabled us to persevere even the most unspeakable hardships that racial domination has forced upon us as a people. According to noted historian, John Blassingame in his classic book, *The Slave Community*, "The family, while it had no legal existence in slavery, was in actuality one of the most important survival mechanisms for the slave" (151). Resolutely, then, we must learn from our history, the attitude of "the primacy of family for slaves [as outlined] in *The Slave Community*," so that we will not succumb to what we appear to be rapidly approaching today—the ultimate decline of the Black family (Hudson-Weems, *Africana Womanism*, 59).

In order to fully address the most salient issue prohibiting total parity within the Africana community, which is dictated by institutionalized racism as informed by the dominant culture, one must unapologetically acknowledge and resolve the menacing phenomenon of sexism and female victimization, a subject introduced in the previous chapter in particular, but more poignantly dramatized in Sister Souljah's *No Disrespect*. No one has better articulated the interlocutory dynamics of Black male-female relationships and sexism in the Black community. The novel opens with a perfect picture of a Black family, seemingly as secure as one can hope for in the "ghetto"—a household with both parents. We observe the very chauvinistic yet protective husband and father, who enjoys being the bread-winner, the wife and mother who was taught to rely totally upon her husband, and the children who enjoy their natural dependency on their parents for everything. All is well until illness befalls the father, who is then forced into retirement, and thus insignificance, since after all, his family and his role is his *raison d'etre*:

> My father was a hardworking man and always had a great love for people. . . . He believed in family. . . He wanted to be a man's man. He believed that it was solely the man's responsibility to bring home the bacon and rule the household. He believed that the woman must work hard at being beautiful, that she make her husband as comfortable as a king in his own castle, that she perfect her skills of housecleaning and cooking and have a lot of babies. After all, he figured, she had all day to correct any flaws in her appearance. Most of all, he demanded that she be fully dependent upon him. No driving, traveling alone, taking classes. No need to think too hard or waste time worrying her pretty little head with survival or business, matters that were properly the province of the man. He must be the source of her money, love, sex, and strength, and the center of her existence. My father was six foot five inches tall, brown-skinned, and had a handsome baby face. (Souljah 5-6)

As times grow harder, he is unable to accept his new status as a dependent, the pressure becomes unbearable, which ultimately leads to the fragile and unpredictable impoverished lives of this somewhat traditional family. A divorce ensues, the mother and children are forced into the projects, and they slowly assume the lifestyle of the inner-city ghetto—crowed slum conditions, mis-education, welfare, promiscuity, drugs, deception, and domestic violence. What sticks in the mind of the protagonist is how her father ultimately succumbs to defeat, a broken man, never to recover his sense of worth:

> My father's visits became irregular. He went from representing one we loved, who disciplined and instructed us, to being something of a loved and favorite clown arriving on intermittent weekends with guilt-filled eyes and broken dreams, filling us up

with endless chocolate bars, Superfly movies, hot dogs, and toys. On the last evening that I was to see him for a while, he arrived with a picture of a crying clown. He told us to hang it on our wall. And when we looked at it, we should think of him, because that's who I am." (Sister Souljah 8-9)

Too frequently, Africana men are guilty of both physically and mentally abusing their women, an unfortunate reality to which, as painful and embarrassing as it is, we have to admit. To say that this dominant practice of female subjugation and victimization is rooted in Africana male experiences of assimilation—e.g., duplicating how white men relate to "their" women—is to take the first step in dismantling the dividing elements in Black male-female relationships that make it difficult for Africana people to unite. Admittedly, the past and current dilemma of the insecurity of Black males, and the plight of Africana men could very well be responsible for causing them to feel that they must physically rule over their female counterparts in order to establish their sense of manhood. However, whether or not they feel justified in their insistence upon male domination, often suspecting that Africana women are out to destroy them, which they believe is the underlining mission of the dominant culture, this disturbing and intimidating reality must stop so that we can once and for all end the vicious cycle that ultimately destroy the Africana family.

The theory of Africana womanism, which addresses the tripartite plight of race, class, and gender of Africana women, particularly as it relates to their families, including their male counterparts, has always condemned the abuse and disrespect of Africana women. Understandably, it would be rather difficult for Africana women to embrace or to promote a collective male-female assault on racial oppression as a primary concern when they are being both physically and verbally abused by their male counterparts at the same time. In other words, it is not easy for Africana women to think of their male counterparts as partners in a liberation struggle when they inflict pain on their women in so many ways, on a daily basis, thereby impeding working together amicably on equal ground. This is certainly not to say that men are the only culprits in this regard; women, too, are often guilty of emotionally and, though surprisingly, physically abusing their men as well. With this in mind, it becomes clear that both the Africana man and the Africana woman must end the disregard and disrespect of each other so that the Africana race can move forward more effectively for our ultimate survival.

It is important at this time to point out that unfortunately there are women who participate in the subjugation inflicted upon them. Often without resistance, they submit to their male partners, granting them either overt or covert permission to abuse them physically and/or mentally, an act of compliance with this age-long senseless practice. They enter into abusive relationships over and over again, wherein they duplicate a pathetic pattern of disrespect and abuse. But this certainly need not be the case. To paraphrase one of our greatest civil rights leaders of all times, Dr. Martin Luther King, Jr., unless you lie down, no one can step on you. And so it is that Black women are going to have to call a halt to this practice by refusing to tolerate any form of abuse, be it physical or otherwise.

In the course of this compelling autobiography, Sister Souljah experiences many disappointments in a number of bad relationships as she searches for her Mr. Right. We painfully witness her "many attempt to find the right man with whom she can have a passionate, sincere, non-threatening, disease-free relationship. She fails each time, not because of her shortcomings alone, but because of the pathologies that black men have acquired from childhood" (Maxwell, *Book Reviews*). As for her mistakes, it seemed that she keeps making the same choices in men. She is too trusting of them, and although past relationships indicate that she needs to ask questions, she takes whatever the men in her life say as truth. For example, one common trait that her male counterparts share is lying about other relationships. According to them, they either do not have other relationships or they do not love the women with whom they are involved, which she accepts as valid reasons for her to get involved with them.

A young freshman in college, Sister Souljah meets and falls in love with a very intelligent and impressive activist, Nathan, whom she not only loves but, more important, trusts and respects. As an activist, in addition to understanding and operating in a leadership capacity in the Black liberation struggle, he also has great insights into the true nature of Black womanhood, which is interconnected with Black manhood, as both command a reciprocal respect between each other.

Echoing the essence of Africana womansim, he insists that "If black women want to be respected . . . they have to respect themselves. He said that we must divorce ourselves from the white society's definition and description of womanhood and present ourselves in a light where a man can get to know our minds instead of just 'running through' our bodies" (Souljah 60). This is truly Africana womanist thinking, as two of the eighteen characteristics of Africana womanism are self-respect and self-definition. Ostensibly, Nathan seems to be a perfect mate for her; however, as the story unfolds, he greatly disappoints her by abandoning her for lengthy periods of time because of psychological issues originating from his early childhood experiences that altered his life and desires forever. As a young boy, his older sister introduced him to her friend David, who, unbeknownst to her, "liked little black boys" (114). Consequently, "instead of loving women who didn't seem to love me, or have anything decent to say, I loved David, the first person to tell me anything positive about myself at a young and impressionable age. By the time women started to admire me and my blackness, my mind was already twisted and I couldn't relate. I was confused and looking for help. . . . I was taught to look at men in a perverted way and women in a negative way" (114-115). When she asks how he feels about the fact that homosexuality won in the end, he says "It's racism. . . . Black Nate, Nate the spade. You so black you blue. Who can see you. Yeah, I liked women like every other young brother does. But women didn't love me. I was always a joke, a crack, a snap" (114). But what is missing here in his analysis is the responsibility of Blacks to reject negative threats to our image of ourselves. We must dismiss, and even topsy-turvey established standards which deny our existence in a positive light, such as what Morrison prescribes in *The Bluest Eye* for the survival of her protagonist, Pecola Breedlove. Thus, as Samuels and Hudson-Weems contends, "Morrison is interested in having the characters achieve a more authentic existence than those who submit to conventional standards, one that emerges from their personal efforts to realize their responsibility to become fulfilled individuals" (10).

The next relationship she has is with Joseph, a married man who, like Nate, was an activist and a spokesman for his people. He does everything to prove to her that he loves her, in spite of his marital and parental status. However, when Sister Souljah tells him she is pregnant with his child, he responds, "Get an abortion" (196). In that one final statement, he implies to her that it is over for them and he then resumes his commitment to his wife and two children.

Between the relationship with Joseph and the third unsuccessful relationship with Chance, short for Terrance, Sister Souljah recounts her younger sister's abusive relationship with her baby's father Leon. She advises her sister to think not only about herself and her personal needs and desires as dictated by "love and affection," a predilection not always in her best interest, but she encourages her to consider her child and what she herself, as a human being, really needs. She summarizes the dilemma of Black women trying to avoid being alone and lonely, rather than insisting on having a good man: "Many times as women we feel we need a man. And, the truth of the matter is, we do need a man. But we need a good man. A bad man is not worth the trouble. It's all right to struggle with a brother to work together to make a better future, to help him out, but physical abuse can never be tolerated under any circumstances" (206). This passage echoes and explains the fundamental concept of Africana womanism, which discourages "merely settling for companionship for the sake of having a man" (Hudson-Weems, *Africana Womanism*, 67). Further, the concept also holds that loving and supporting your male counterpart does not mean that you allow him to physically and emotionally abuse and disrespect you. While demanding that he respects you, you must also give him respect, a practice that should be handed down as an empowering legacy for your children to emulate. This, in deed, would be a positive model for future generations, enabling them to break the cycle of hate and self-deprecation.

She also discusses the life and lifestyle of her friend Mona, a lesbian who erroneously believes same-sex relationships are more secure. Dispelling this myth, Sister Souljah says the following:

> From the looks of things, Mona, you've been hurt by some guy from the past. Since you don't confide in me that will always be a mystery to me. But somehow you've allowed that experience to turn you off to all men. But sleeping with a woman does not guarantee you anything. Women, too, can be power-hungry exploiters. Women, too, can be two-timing low-down

cheats. Women, too, can be emotionally abusive and
insensitive. I mean, damn, Mona. I been stood up. Me
by a man. You by a woman. I been lied to. You been
lied to. I been lonely, you been lonely. But guess what?
It doesn't matter how good you can make me feel,
Mona. When I think about it, I imagine there are a lot
of things that can make me feel good. Maybe you
could bring me some level of sexual pleasure. So could
a lot of people and a lot of things. That doesn't make
it right, though. (223)

The dialogue continues for a while, with Mona justifying her "bitter
anti-male sentiment, leading to a thoroughgoing cynicism toward life.
She wasn't alone. There seemed to be a growing number of college
girls who shared this outlook. Many, like Mona, had embraced a gay
lifestyle" (212-213). But Sister Souljah is unyielding in her position.
Finally, she summarizes her beliefs as follows: "Look at it like a math-
ematical equation. If everyone were to adopt the gay lifestyle, the end
result would be the death of the entire community because the so-
called gay lifestyle cannot produce life. Two men can't make a baby
any more than two women can" (224). Thus, "...male and female relationships are not only comforting but the key to perpetuating the
human race. Without each other, the human race becomes extict
(Hudson-Weems, *Africana Womanism*, 67). She ultimately resigns herself to the fact that Mona will not change her opinions:

Mona, all I have to offer you is sisterhood. Real sisterhood. The kind I offer my own blood sisters. It's
what makes me able to work hard and sacrifice to
keep another woman from feeling that same pain I
felt or the pain of our ancestors. But what it isn't for
me is sexual. That's a wrong turn. It's an irrational
response to a very complex question. You should
understand what that means. If you want to understand Brooklyn and the many confused dark people,
you should realize how it has scarred the men and
the women to the point where we've even forgotten
how to love one another. But what I can't do is do

what other people are doing just because they fig-
ured out a way to make it look right. (225)

The chapter entitled Chance is one of the most riveting in the whole
book. It opens with Tusani, a pathetic twelve-year-old prostitute, who
obviously comes from a dysfunctional family. She lives in one of the
inner-city "welfare hotels," one that breeds female vulnerability, exploitation, and victimization. Living in a single parent household, she is con-
demned by an abusive mother, Nita, who has two other children, Charelle
and Ray-Ray. When Sister Souljah befriends this child out of a great
compassion for her people, particularly for the children in the Black
community, she demonstrates what it really means to love and protect
a child. In attempting to give little Tusani a sense of security and to raise
her self-esteem, she takes her to her apartment, gives her a key to the
apartment should she ever need someplace to retreat to, and even takes
her shopping—all of which Tusani's mother strongly disapproves:

> "Where the fuck did you get all that shit from?...
> "She bought it for me."
> "Did you ask her for it?"
> "No, I didn't ask her for nothing'. She just bought
> if for me." Then I heard a smack and a noise which
> was probably Tusani falling to the floor.
> "Bitch! Don't you get smart with me! I'll knock
> all your damn teeth down your throat." . . . Suddenly,
> the door was snatched open. Nita stood there wide-
> eyed and mean-faced, looking nothing like the
> woman I had met outside the other day. She had one
> hand on her hip with her neck working overtime as
> she proceeded to put me in my place. "Look. Let me
> tell you what the problem is. You go out and buy
> Tusani all this shit. Then I gotta deal with her little
> fucked-up attitude when she thinks she's cute up in
> here. You don't know Tusani. You just met her. She's
> a smart-ass little tricky bitch."
> "Ma! . . . Tusani attempted to interrupt.
> "How the hell is you gonna talk when I'm already
> talking? See, that's what I mean. She forgets who the

hell's in charge around here. . . . Now what is I'm supposed to do when Charelle and Ray-Ray get back
home and they ain't got shit and you bought Tusani
all of this shit? . . . I want you to remember one thing.
Tusani is black. She ain't nothin' but a black nigga.
She ain't no princess bitch. She's a nigga just like
everybody else around here and she was born to suffer.
She don't need no special treatment and she sure don't
deserve none. Now, you take this and you can go."
(248-249)

Clearly Tusani comes out of a violent, cold, and loveless environment.
She doesn't know what it means to be truly loved and cared for by an
adult. It is no wonder then she falls prey to a despicable, disgusting
older pimp whose smooth talking represents the only words of ten-
derness and approval she can ever hope to receive in such an environment. He makes her believe that he has rescued her from the depths
of child abuse, poverty, and degradation; that without him she has
nothing upon which to depend :

> "Now who took plain Vanessa and gave her a
> new look and a new name?' . . .
> "You did, Try-Love."
> "Now when I turned Vanessa into Queen
> Khadijah, didn't I introduce you to a life of royalty?
> Didn't I fatten up your pockets? . . . If the Queen still
> loves me—and I hope she does—she's gonna do what
> makes me happy. She's gonna charm these dudes with
> her beauty, make 'em feel real good with that young
> body and those juicy lips. Then she's gonna bring those
> green bills back to Daddy so he can personally show
> her his appreciation. Now, what's my name, Queen?"
> "Try Love," she said proudly. He grabbed her butt
> cheek and flashed a smile, asking her like a gentle-
> man, "Well then, shall we?" He extended his arm and
> she tucked hers in his. And to my amazement they
> walked off together, both looking satisfied and ready.
> (228-229)

As if Tusani's pathetic life of abuse and disappointments is not enough, Sister Souljah meets with yet another unsuccessful relationship, this time with the selfish and deceptive Chance, a manipulating con artist who has her believing that Angela, his wife and the mother of his little boy, is neither his wife nor the love of his life. His style alone, smooth talking and overconfident, should have been enough to warn her that she was going in the wrong direction. Moreover, his name, too, should have suggested that she was taking a big chance on him, especially since he was forever borrowing money from her to help him in questionable situations. In the end, he abandons Sister Souljah, revealing as he does his deceitful and lying ways in his final gesture to secure his marriage after his wife forces him to tell the truth and admit that his extramarital relationship with Sister Souljah was all a game for money. Love and sex, Chance tells her, were never to have been a part of the game. Coldly dropping Sister Souljah, he informs her that "I don't love you and I never did" (306).

The book culminates in her relationship with a man named Derek with whom she shares her musical talents. He comes up with an idea as to how they can successfully mesh their talents:

> "I think your voice and what you have to say to our people needs to be heard. If we took pieces of your speeches and put them on top of some hard beats, I think we would have a hit." I was fascinated by the idea of mixing political-historical speeches over hip-hop beats. It seemed like a step in the right direction toward the media projects I was interested in creating. Derek said he would produce the music if I would do the lyrics. . . . He explained that we would both benefit: He would get a break as a producer; I would get to explore a new and powerful arena as a performing artist. (319)

This was only the beginning for them. As time went on, they began to connect on an intimate level. While she was not in love with him, the fact that he was a smart and caring person who wanted to have a relationship with her made her interested. He, for one, did at least, admit that he was currently in a relationship, one that had gone on for nearly a decade. However, he had her believe initially that he was not in love with this lady, Trina, but rather remained involved with her because of his early childhood of having been abandoned by his father, thereby making it difficult for him to abandon another. He suggested instead a polygamist relationship with the three of them, to which she agreed. To justify entering a shared relationship, she reasons that she not only solves the problem of male deception, as they often lie about their involvement with other women, but that she solves the problem of male shortage: "The sharing thing was a political decision on my part because of the genocide, the man-shortage problem" (346). She thought that if we could be up front with our relationships, then there would be no reason to lie. She wanted Trina to agree to this arrangement, but her attempt was thwarted. It took her dear friend Sheri to put it all into proper perspective, critiquing her proposal for a polygamist rela-tionship and disclosing the shortcomings of such an arrangement:

> Bullshit! . . . The sharing thing doesn't make any sense. It's not even logical. It's unlike you to be illogical. You're saying that you know these men out here are dysfunctional? . . . So you're asking a dysfunctional man who cannot properly manage and conduct one successful relationship with one woman, to conduct two relationships with two women? It's impossible. If you can't handle and love and support one, how can you handle and love and support two? . . . Chance not only broke your heart, he destroyed your ego. . . . No sister in love is gonna sit down and discuss sharing the love of her life. That's why Trina can't do it. . . . Girl, you and I will find strong men. But it will take time. They're scarce. But in the meantime, girl, you can't get desperate. Desperate women settle for anything. They lower their standards and all the dogs come wan-dering in. (345-347)

Thanks to the genuine sisterhood that exists between the persona and her friend girl Sheri, that she was able to change her direction.

In her grand finale, Listen Up! (Straighten It Out), Sister Souljah has clearly gotten herself together, as she comes all the way back to her true Africana roots as a positive political activist. She accurately sums up the major problems confronting Blacks in America:

> Too many of us are in pain; too many of us are lonely. Sex is everywhere while true love falls victim to the turmoil of our fight merely to survive. Racism is a disease. It affects whites as well as blacks. It may even be a kind of mental illness. But the effect on black people is greater because we are the victims of it. The effect on whites is severe because it deforms their thinking and gives them a distorted picture of the world. (349)

She concludes that our only salvation in through the survival of the Black family, which depends upon responsibility and positive Black male-female relationships. Her answer to her penultimate question, "Can African male-female relationships survive in America?" (350), inadvertently challenges the Black community:

> Not if black-on-black love is dead. Not if we are still too scared to admit there is a problem while our families fall apart. Not if our young men continue to refer to young women as "bitches." Or our young women refer to young men as 'motherfuckers,' or all of us refer to each other as "niggas." It is a sad measure of our profound contempt for each other and of our thoroughgoing self-loathing that we continue to persist in this ugly practice. (350)

As the book comes to a close, Sister Souljah offers invaluable suggestions for our survival. She urges us to prepare our children to survive and to consider the nature of entrapment that welfare offers its recipients with its false sense of security. If indeed one must use this means of survival, it should only be on a temporary basis. Like a true Africana womanist, she reiterates that Africana women define themselves, and that they demonstrate love and compassion for their male counterparts, at the same time demanding respect and proper treatment from them. She also cautions women against dating their girlfriends' men, as well as dating married men, who can only bring you woe in the final analysis: "Do not mess with a married man. He will take your sex and go back to his wife. You will end up crying and in pain. Moreover, by messing with a married man you will be helping to destroy a family, an African family, which already is struggling to survive. To steal away with the father of someone else's children is wrong" (356–357). For women who feel that men in general are bad because they abuse women, that their options are limited, and that their time is running out, she cautions against concluding that "same-sex love will solve your problems. . . . [because] women are abusers just like men" (357). Believing that "a real man respects his women," she then takes us back to a spiritual level, as she had early on confessed that "my strength was my relationship with God and my ability to think and pray" (Souljah 34). Spirituality, one of the elements of Africana womanism, again reins high in her life: "I believe in God. I believe God is spirit and the power of God lives in the soul of every boy and girl, man and woman" (357, 359). Ultimately Sister Souljah concludes, "God gave us minds with which to think. Remember. No one will save us but ourselves. Neither God nor white people will do so. But first we must learn to respect ourselves. That is the test we must pass, the promise we must make to each other, the challenge of all of our lives" (360). Adhering to these recommendations, we could then appreciate the inevitable: "The end result would be that Africana people (men and women) the world over would then collectively struggle toward recovering their natural birthright as determiners of their fate as liberated people, dedicated to their families and their future generations (Hudson-Weems, *Africana Womanism*, 144).

Chapter VIII

Morrison's Beloved: All Parts Equal[1]

> She is a friend of my mind. She gather me, man. The
> pieces I am, she gather them and give them back to
> me in all the right order. It's good, you know, when
> you got a woman who is a friend of your mind.[2]
> (Morrison *Beloved*)

The key to understanding a positive Africana man-woman relationship is described in Toni Morrison's *Beloved* in the assessment of the relationship of a male character named Sixo and his woman, the
Thirty-Mile Woman. This is significant, for Morrison, like many Africana
woman novelists, demonstrates definite growth and development in
her characterization of both men and women. Of particular importance
is the demonstration of her female characters acute awareness of their
interaction with their family and their community. This becomes obvious as Morrison concentrates not only on the reality of Africana life
and culture—its richness, its strengths, and its weaknesses—but, more
important, on that community's strategies for survival in the concerted
struggle of the men and women in the ever-existing battle against
racism.

From her first novel, *The Bluest Eye*, to *Sula, Song of Solomon, Tar
Baby*, and finally to her fifth novel, *Beloved* (1987), Morrison developed the male and the female roles in this collective struggle. According
to Mbalia in Toni Morrison's *Developing Class Consciousness*, "*Beloved*
. . . examines a critical historical period in the African's life in order
primarily to demonstrate that African people have and thus can sur-

vive the most oppressive conditions by collectively struggling against them. . . . African people can survive their present day crisis through organization" (27).

Hence, in Morrison's *Beloved*, Paul D and Sethe struggle for family unity through the guidance of the "unchurched preacher" Baby Suggs, Holy at the clearing (a place where they congregate in a ritual setting) to love, claim, and redefine themselves, and of the community of women, in spite of their differences with Sethe, who comes near the end of the novel to rid her of the evil ghost, Beloved, through an exorcism. All this and more bear out the notion of the undeniable significance of communal struggle for the survival of the Africana family.

The focal point for Morrison's writing is the woman, the culture bearer, who must operate within the constructs of her own culture in order to lead an authentic existence. According to Samuels and Hudson-Weems:

> The authentic individual in Morrison's world realizes that his or her rights, duties, and responsibilities in the neighborhood of human kind are to act, to choose. The individual must realize the absolute freedom to choose. [141]

And for Sethe, the ultimate responsibility is to her children. Her decision to murder them (she succeeds in killing only one—Beloved) rather than have them experience the "unspeakable" evils of slavery, of which she herself is well aware, demonstrates that responsibility. This depiction of the Africana woman in her commitment to her children and her family is present to some degree in all of Morrison's novels, but the true Africana womanist culminates in the Morrison canon with *Beloved*.

Beginning with *The Bluest Eye*, Morrison's first novel, we see the Africana womanist to evolve in the character of the child narrator, Claudia, who embodies authenticity. Unlike the other little girls, who accept the white standard of beauty and love white baby dolls, Claudia, in her rejection of the "ideal beauty," confesses:

> I was physically revolted by and secretly frightened of those round moronic eyes, the pancake face, and

orangeworms hair. The other dolls, which were supposed to bring me great pleasure, succeeded in doing
quite the opposite. [20]

A self-definer, Claudia accepts her own perspective regarding the standard of beauty relative to her culture.

In the second novel, *Sula*, the character most representative of the
Africana womanist is Eva Peace, the grandmother of the title character. Both self-defined and family-centered, Eva is the supreme mother,
one who loves her children, so much that she sacrifices one of her legs
in order to collect insurance money in order to take care of them.
Thus, as Samuels and Hudson-Weems contend, "Eva (Eve) provides the
ideal, for she is the archetypal 'Great Mother'" [38]. But for Eva the role
of mother does not limit itself to her children. It extends itself to the
entire community, for she cares for her granddaughter, the orphaned
Dewey boys, and others in her community who need her assistance in
any way.

In *Song of Solomon*, Pilate is the true Africana womanist. A pariah
and the granddaughter of the legendary Solomon, the African who
could fly, Pilate has a positive sense of her African ancestry, which was
handed down to her by her father, Jake. Like Eva, Pilate defines life
for herself and hers. But unlike her brother Macon, Sr., who believes
that material things in life are superior to spiritual and cultural things,
she leads a truly authentic existence, one in which her historical and
cultural self supersedes, and in an African tradition, she passes the legacy
of her rich ancestry on to her nephew Milkman, who, like herself,
may come to appreciate to live an authentic existence in his beliefs
and actions.

In order to identify the Africana womanist in *Tar Baby*, one must
look to the community of women. Here we find a collective character that comes later in the novel, in the women's attempt to nurture one
of the protagonists, Jadine, who is the supreme example of inauthenticity: "the night women simply want to nurse Jadine into a healthy
mental attitude toward her culture" (Samuels and Hudson-Weems
91). Like the Africana womanist, the community of women collectively serves as nurturer and culture-bearer. Though the women must
join their race in the struggle for existence, they, as true Africana
women, must insist that the lives of their people be both authentic

and holistic.

It is in the author's fifth novel, *Beloved*, that we witness the author's supreme Africana womanist characters—Sethe and Baby Suggs. But Morrison goes further. For the first time, she fully develops a whole and completely positive male character, Paul D—in concert with a female companion—who clearly represents the flip side of the coin, the Africana man. While Sethe, Baby Suggs, and Paul D collectively represent the sum total of a true Africana persona. But the true Africana womanist is the focus here, for she is one who demonstrates the following positive attributes: self-namer and self-definer, family-centered, female companion in collective struggle, strong, spiritual, respectful of elders, holistic, authentic, and nurturing. It must be noted that the lives of these major characters are intricately intertwined with the lives of others in the community. Thus, they are concerned with more than themselves; for it is only with a sense and appreciation of others that an Africana womanist is able to find true meaning in life.

Early in the novel, Morrison depicts Sethe as one who has learned that "She had claimed herself. Freeing yourself was one thing; claiming ownership of that freed self was another" (*Beloved* 95). But it is much more than self that she is concerned about. A family-centered woman with strong maternal instincts, the welfare of her children is of utmost importance to her. For the dignity of having her deceased child's name, Beloved, placed on her tombstone, for example, Sethe sacrifices herself, having sex with the engraver in exchange for an inscription? "'Ten minutes,' he said 'You got ten minutes. I'll do it for free. Ten minutes for seven letter'" (5). Later, after her escape from the Sweet Home Plantation, when she is reunited with her children "Sethe lay in bed under, around, over, among, but especially with them all" (93). There is no doubt that Sethe loves her children, so much so that she is willing to kill them all rather than have them enslaved and experience what she as a slave woman had experienced—"the unspeakable." Declaring her great love for her children, she says:

> I have felt what it felt like and nobody walking or
> stretched out is going to make you feel it too. Not
> you, not one of mine, and when I tell you you mine,
> I also mean I'm yours. I wouldn't draw breath with-
> out my children. [203]

In demonstrating the collective male-female struggle and companionship, Morrison focuses on the relationship between Sethe and Paul D, which is based upon a shared history and mutual respect. In attempting to convince Sethe that they could have a beautiful future together, Morrison writes:

> Sethe, if I'm here with you, with Denver, you can go
> anywhere you want. Jump, if you want to, 'cause I'll
> catch you, girl. I'll catch you 'fore you fall. Go as far
> inside as you need to, I'll hold your ankles. Make sure
> you get back out. . . . I have been heading in this direc-
> tion for seven year. . . . I knew it wasn't this place I
> was heading toward; it was you. We can make a life,
> girl. A life. [46]

It does not take long for Sethe to realize that Paul D is, in fact, an agent for her healing: "She knew Paul D was adding something to her life. . . . Now he added more: new pictures and old rememories that broke her heart" (95). They become one, for together they can transcend their painful past as fellow slaves.

Sethe and Paul D unquestionably share a common bond, as "her story was bearable because it was his as well—to tell, to refine and tell again" (99). They'd been victimized in similar ways—both used as work horses and abused as grantees to the sexual whims of their oppressors. As readers are well aware that the women in *Beloved* represent the victims of "the 'unspeakable' fate to which most female slaves were heiresses," so are readers aware that this fate is one not experienced by the slave woman alone (Samuels and Hudson-Weems 94). On the contrary, Africana men, too, experienced sexual exploitation by their slave holders, thereby validating this author's thesis that sexual exploitation and racism more closely identify the dynamics of the Africana experience during slavery than does the notion of sexual exploitation and gender. One need only pit one of Sethe's experiences of sexual exploitation with one of Paul D's to demonstrate the commonality of their victimization. The following is a conversation between Sethe and Paul D, describing both the violation of her womanhood and her humanity.

"They used cowhide on you?"
"And they took my milk."
"They beat you and you was pregnant?"
"And they took my milk." [17]

The oppressor both physically brutalized her and, in "stealing" her milk, deprived her child of food.

Now here is the story behind what made Paul D tremble. Paul D was sent to Georgia to work on a chain gang for attempting to kill his new slave master. He recounts his deplorable experience there, including those of his fellow workers who were placed in situations in which they were forced to grant white oppressors sexual favors.

> Chain-up completed, they knelt down. . . . Kneeling in the mist they waited for the whim of a guard, or two, or three. Or maybe all of them wanted it. Wanted it from one prisoner in particular or none—or all.
> "Breakfast? Want some breakfast, nigger?"
> "Yes, sir."
> "Hungry, nigger?"
> "Yes, sir."
> "Here you go."
> Occasionally a kneeling man chose gunshot in his head as the price, maybe, of taking a bit of fore-skin with him to Jesus. Paul did not know that then. He was looking at his palsied hands, swelling the guard, listening to his soft grunts so like the doves', as he stood before the man kneeling in mist on his right. Convinced he was next, Paul retched—vomiting up nothing at all. An observing guard smashed his shoulder with the rifle and the engaged one decided to skip the new man for the time being lest his pants and shoes got soiled by nigger puke. [107-108]

The common plight of both Sethe and Paul D is a case in point of the oneness of Africana men and women in the sense of a common history and a common struggle for survival, one that far exceeds the commonality of the feminist struggle of women in general against female subjugation. Sethe and Paul D represent the concerted struggle of Africana men and women.

Toward the end of the novel, the two come to an agreement. Paul D offers this commitment to work toward creating a better life for the two of them, and Sethe seems certain to accept it: "He wants to put his story next to hers. 'Sethe,' he says, 'me and you, we got more yesterday than anybody. We need some kind of tomorrow'" (273). With Paul D's assistance, Sethe can now begin to appreciate herself. Paul D tells her, "'You your best thing, Sethe. You are'" (273).

Another element of the Africana womanist is that of spirituality. In this novel, the author lures readers into the magical world of her characters, where ghosts are alive and physically interact with the living. Mysticism and spirituality, Samuels and Hudson-Weems have observed, are so much a part of Morrison's world:

> Morrison's spellbinding prose/poetry ("Sifting daylight dissolves the memory, turns it into dust motes floating in the light" [*Beloved* 264]), coupled with the mysticism, black folklore, and mythology woven into her fictional worlds have lead many critics to append the label "Black Magic" to her craftsmanship. Beginning with her first novel, she has captivated audiences with such conjured worlds as Medallion and the Bottom, Darling and Not Doctor Streets, Isles de Chevaliers, and most recently 124 Bluestone Road, places where blackbirds appear unexpectedly, family remains are kept indoors unburied, warrior spirts gallop on horseback, and a ghost becomes flesh and blood. Even the names of her characters work like charms: Pecola and Cholly Breedlove, Eva and Sula Peace, Pilate and Milkman Dead, Shadrack, Guitar, Son, Jadine, Sethe, Paul D, Stamp Paid, Baby Suggs, and Beloved. [ix-x]

From the author's debut novel to her most recent one, spirituality reigns:

There is, for example, Soaphead Church, a spiritualist who uses magic to ostensibly grant Pecola her
desired blue eyes in *The Bluest Eye*. There is Eva's
dream book of numbers, her superstitions about
attending a wedding in a red dress and about the flock
of blackbirds that marked Sula's return to the Bottom,
and Ajax's conjuring mother in *Sula*. There is the
navelless shaman Pilate who keeps her dead father's
bones in her house and communicates with the dead
in *Song of Solomon*. And there are the visitations experienced by Valerian Street in *Tar Baby*. [Samuels and
Hudson-Weems 135]

None of these works, however, develops this theme so dramatically as
does *Beloved*. The very existence of the title character in this novel
evolves magically:

A fully dressed woman walked out of the water. She
barely gained the dry bank of the stream before she
sat down and leaned against a mulberry tree. All day
and all night she sat there, her head resting on the
trunk in a position abandoned enough to crack the
brim in her straw hat. . . . Nobody saw her emerge
or came accidentally by. If they had, chances are they
would have hesitated before approaching her. Not
because she was wet . . . but because amid all that she
was smiling. . . . She had new skin, lineless and smooth,
including the knuckles of her hands. [50]

Although it is obvious at the outset that the woman is mysterious, the
extent of her powers becomes more apparent as time passes on. When
Paul D asks the strange newcomer her name, she responds "Beloved,"
but the response is in a voice that "was so low and rough each one
looks at the other two. They heard the voice first—later the name"
(52). But unlike the ghosts in other Morrison works, Beloved has physical contact with the living characters. She implants her destructive
spirit and power, for example, into her grandmother Baby Suggs (Sethe's

mother-in-law). Here the spirit of Beloved directs her revenge upon her mother for killing her:

> The fingers touching the back of her neck were stronger now—the strokes bolder as though Baby Suggs were gathering strength. Putting the thumbs at the nape, while the fingers pressed the sides. Harder, harder, the fingers moved slowly around toward her wind-pipe, making little circles on the way. Sethe was actually more surprised than frightened to find that she was being strangled. Or so it seemed. In any case, Baby Suggs' fingers had a grip on her that would not let her breathe. Tumbling forward from her seat on the rock, she clawed at the hands that were not there. Her feet were thrashing by the time Denver got to her. [96]

Not only does Beloved—a shape-shifter who is able to change her form from baby to twenty-one-years-old woman—have a physical encounter with her mother, Sethe, she vengefully engages in an affair with Sethe's lover, Paul D. He cannot understand the power she possesses, the power that compels him to have sex with her against his will and better judgment. His rationalizations about sleeping with this girl have merit in his reality, but he would scarcely be able to convince Sethe. He thinks thoughts he cannot bring himself to verbalize. Practicing what he would like to admit to Sethe, however, he says:

> "It ain't a weakness, the kind of weakness I can fight 'cause something is happening to me, that girl is doing it, I know you think I never liked her nohow, but she is doing it to me. Fixing me. Sethe, she's fixed me and I can't break it." [127]

Just as Beloved is able to enter the mind and body of Baby Suggs, hereby controlling her actions, she is also able to enter Paul D's mind and body, making him respond to her the way she wants, helping her get revenge on her mother. Indeed, the living and the living dead come together to carry out the action in this narrative.

Later in the novel, we learn that Beloved has no lines in her hands, a folk–belief indication that she is a ghost. This is revealed in a conversation between Ms. Janey Wagon and Denver, who is seeking work to help her ailing mother manage the household and to assist in caring for their "visitor."

> "Tell me, this here woman in your house. The cousin. She got any lines in her hands?"
> "No," said Denver.
> "Well," said Janey. "I guess there's a God after all." [254]

There is another level of spirituality in the novel, unrelated to ghosts, but to the inexplicable powers of the living. Sethe talks about the magic surrounding Denver, her living daughter:

> "Nothing bad can happen to her. Look at it. Everybody I knew dead or gone or dead and gone. Not her. Not my Denver. Even when I was carrying her, when it got clear that I wasn't going to make it— which meant she wasn't going to make it either—she pulled a whitegirl out of the hill. The last thing you'd expect to help. And when the schoolteacher found us and came busting in here with the law and a shotgun . . . I wasn't going back there. I don't care who found who. Any life but not that one. I went to jail instead. Denver was just a baby so she went right along with me. Rats bit everything in there but her." [42]

A mysterious power engulfs Denver, protects her, even controls her survival. Even before her birth she was shielded against all dangers and threats to her life. Despite Beloved's intrusions and attacks, Denver survives. Despite Beloved's ability to alienate Sethe from Denver (who loves and fears her mother with equal intensity), Denver survives. Her magical protective shield, as real and powerful as anything else in the universe, embraces her, enabling her to withstand the common and not-so-common dangers in life.

There seems yet another level of spirituality operating for the Africana womanist in *Beloved*. While spirituality as interpreted earlier

124

reflects more the mystical quality, there are instances of spirituality in the novel that reflect the power to heal. And that is exactly the power Baby Suggs possesses. Her daughter-in-law Sethe escapes slavery to join her in Ohio and arrives in a terrible physical state. She must be healed to pull through, and it is, of course, Baby Suggs who nurtures her back to good health, giving her herbs and rubbing her body, her feet in particular, to bring her out of her pain. Much in the same tradition as "the laying on of hands" that many spiritualist use in healing the sick, Baby Suggs does a sort of "laying on of words," if you will, in healing the minds and attitudes of the people in her family and community. Deemed the "unchurched preacher," she goes to the "Clearing," an open area in the woods, and leads her people in a nontraditional sermon, teaching them the power of loving themselves in order to save themselves:

> "Here," she said, "in this here place, we flesh; flesh that weeps, laughs; flesh that dances on bear feet in grass. Love it. Love it hard. Yonder they do not love your flesh. They despise it. They don't love our eyes; they'd just as soon pick en out. No more do they love the skin on your back. Yonder they flay it. And O my people they do not love your hands. Those they only use, tie, bind, chop off and leave empty. Love your hands! Love them. Raise them up and kiss them.... And all your inside parts that they'd just as soon slop for hogs, you got to love them. The dark, dark liver— love it, love it, and the beat and beating heart, love that too. More than eyes or feet. More than lungs that have yet to draw free air. More than your life-holding womb and your life-giving private parts, hear me now, love your heart. For this is the prize." [88–89]

Baby Suggs emerges, as a giving Africana womanist, whose concern for her entire family, the Africana community, is her ultimate purpose in life.

A kind of universal mother for Africana humankind, Baby Suggs successfully fulfills her role as nurturer, spiritualist, and activist for her people—the greatest attributes of an Africana womanist. Sethe, too, fulfills her role in life. Like Baby Suggs, she is consistent in her love and commitment to her family. While many may disagree with her methods of protecting her children—she slashes Beloved's throat in her tender act of mercy killing to spare the tot from the horrors of slavery—none can truly believe that Sethe did not act out of true love. In an interview with Charlene Hunter Galt,[2] Morrison herself contends that while Sethe did what was right [which was acting in good faith by taking her child out of the misery of slavery through death], she did not have the right to kill Beloved. To be sure, the Africana womanist reigns high in these two admirable characters, Sethe and Baby Suggs. They are undaunted in their sense of family and community (including the inclination toward positive male companionship), and they exude a tremendous sense of spirituality and nurturing that unquestionably makes them truly authentic in their ongoing quest for wholeness through freedom.

Notes

1. This chapter is excerpted from Clenora Hudson-Weem's *Africana Womanism: Reclaiming Ourselves.*
2. Toni Morrison, *Beloved* (New York: Alfred A. Knopf, 1987), 272-273. All subsequent references to this novel will come from this printing.
3. Interview with Charlene Hunter Gault, "MacNeil/Lehrer News & World Report."

Bibliography

Mbalia, Doreatha Drummond. *Toni Morrison's Developing Class Consciousness.* Selinsgrove, Pa.: Susquehanna University Press, 1991.
Morrison, Toni. *Beloved.* New York: Alfred A. Knopf, 1987.
____. *The Bluest Eye.* New York: Holt, Rinehart, & Winston, 1970.
Samuels, Wilfred, and Clenora Hudson-Weems. *Toni Morrison.* Boston: Prentice-Hall, 1990.

Chapter IX

Beloved: From Novel to Movie[1]

"Enough of that slavery stuff." That was Oprah Winfrey changing the focus, as she continued to do throughout the making of the movie *Beloved*, with a casual dismissal of slavery in a recent television interview with Rosie O'Donnell, admitting that she spent only one of the three days she planned in the wilderness in her preparation for the lead role as Sethe. The film is an adaptation of the 1987 Pulitzer Prize-winning novel by the 1995 Nobel Prize-winning author Toni Morrison. Oprah's statement, reflecting a careless attitude on her part toward a major and defining aspect of African-American life—slavery—sadly represents the mentality of the very people assigned to the serious charge of preserving, interpreting and disseminating the legacy of black people via the most popular and effective media today—visual imagery, the silver screen.

But the movie itself, far beyond what Oprah has to *say* about it, poses more serious problems. To begin with, the title character, Beloved, who upon her physical arrival at 124 Bluestone Road in the novel, recovers the necessary physical and emotional developmental stages she was denied due to her early death. These stages occur early on in the novel, in less than twenty-five pages, in fact, as we witness her grow from a sleeping, drooling infant, to a clumsy, wobbling toddler, to a throwing up, sweets-craving child, and ultimately to the eighteen-year-old young lady, the same age she would have been had she lived, complete with making unwise and immature choices as she begins to move on into adulthood, which unfortunately she is unable to realize before her end. In the movie, however, we find the title character trapped in her recovering developmental stages, thereby rendering her seemingly retarded, which seems to suggest that her condition is a result of her horrible death. A distracting distortion of the novel, Beloved's speech in the film never develops beyond that of a very young babbling child, further erroneously assumed to have resulted from Sethe's cutting her throat with a handsaw, and thereby permanently damaging her voice, and rendering it all the more difficult to evoke total empathy for the mother in her deed. In the novel, on the other hand, Beloved's speech, like her sense of sexuality in her seduction of Paul D, gravitates to a more mature level, while throughout the movie, she is unable to do even the base things for herself, like eating and eliminating properly. In the movie, she is also unable to perform what is assumed to come easy and natural for black people—dancing, while Morrison's portrayal of the title character shows her moving with a "slide and strut on down. . . [with] her fists on her hips . . . [as] her black skirt swayed from side to side." She has obviously mastered the art of dancing, for her sister, Denver, is driven to ask, "Where'd you learn to dance?"

Casting, too, is problematic, particularly in the case of *Beloved*, played by a British actress, Thandie Newton, whose father is British and whose mother is from Zimbabwe, thus without a drop of African-American blood, even though the story is about the African-American slave experience. Thank God for the wonderful casting of Beah Richards and Lisa Gay Hamilton in the movie. The stupendous acting of the former as the powerfully spiritual Baby Suggs is truly "the prize" in the movie, as well as the superb acting of the latter (the younger Sethe), who captivates, at least for that powerful moment in the movie, the essence of a mother's determination to "save" her children from going back into a deplorable slave existence.

There is definitely a downplaying of the primacy of the "ghost" of slavery and its indelible, historical impact on the lives of Black people, in spite of the fact that fear of slavery itself played the deciding role in forcing the mother to choose the ultimate crime of murdering her own child to spare her the "unspeakable" horrors of slavery. Moreover, the ambiguity of Morrison's ghost itself, representing "sixty million and more" who were victims of the horrific slave atrocities, is forever lost in the movie. Hence *Beloved* is tragically reduced to a mere ghost story, with all its physical trappings. Emphasis here is on the vengeful title character's mental and physical limitations after returning from "the other side," rather than on the powerful impact of the institution of slavery. More background and details on slave experiences would have better prepared the audience for at least appreciating Sethe's complicated act, of which Morrison herself asserts that the mother did what was right although she did not have the right to do it. Needless to say, the horrid slave incidents are reduced to scanty, incomprehensible, truncated flashbacks of such significant characters as Schoolteacher, not representative of the fully developed flashbacks characteristic of Morrison novels. Six-o, who represents in the novel the profound love of black men for black women in his relationship with his "Thirty-Mile Woman"—for whom he has to travel thirty miles to another plantation just to spend an hour with her—appears in a quick flash, with barely a name, with barely a history. Significantly as he is lynched in the novel, he defiantly yells "Seven-o," thereby announcing his unborn child, who represents the coming of another black generation. Suggested here is that we don't die, but rather keep on coming, indeed, a powerful commentary on our survival, which is lost in the movie version.

Another significant omission in the movie was Paul D's deplorable experience in Georgia on the chain-gang, which "made him tremble." That experience, the sexual exploitation of black men by white men (guards) forces us to appreciate the commonality of the sexual exploitation of both black men and black women, used as receptacles for white pleasures during slavery. Why such critical historical data is omitted is a mystery, for certainly it could not have been done to accommodate the movie rating. Certainly it was no more revealing than the scene with Beloved, nude with a frontal rather than a profile shot revealing her pubic hair. And certainly, the Georgia scene was no more sexually revealing than the added nude scene with Paul D (Danny Glover) as he rises out of the bathtub to embrace Sethe. This is not to suggest, however, that the love scenes were not good; for Paul D, as in the novel, portrays well the beautiful love for and commitment to black women that black men had even during the hard times of slavery, which we certainly need more of.

Having said all this, some will say that a movie on slavery and even its impact is better than no movie on the subject at all. Granted, but the question remains: Is this movie, like the novel itself, which Morrison dedicates to "Sixty Million and more," really about slavery and its indelible impact on black life? Or is the movie all about the love of a mother for her child? Unquestionably it should be about both and particularly about how slavery transcends the individual, the personal, to an absolute invasion of every aspect of black life—historically, politically, psychologically, economically, socially and physically—forever. Morrison had stated years ago that her intentions in writing the book was to "rip that veil" to tell the whole story of slave life and to present the interior lives of the enslaved themselves. Together, these issues communicate the bigger picture, which unfortunately the movie sorely misses, a short-coming that reflects the inability of most to comprehend, and to communicate to a hungry audience the profound spirituality as well as the physical, emotional, and psychological surroundings of the pervasive, never-ending, debilitating, haunting remnants of true unimaginable horrors of American slavery.

Clenora Hudson-Weems, Ph.D., and her co-author Wilfred Samuels, Ph.D., are recipients of a plaque from the *Toni Morrison Society*, acknowledging the publication of their *Toni Morrison* (1990), the first book on the author, which also includes the first analysis of *Beloved*.

Note

1. This chapter is reprinted with permission from *The Western Journal of Black Studies*, 23 (3), 203-204

Chapter X

Conclusion: Africana Womanism Forever More

About a decade after the 1993 publication of *Africana Womanism: Reclaiming Ourselves*, the sequence to that volume comes forth. *Africana Womanist Literary Theory* offers new insights in the theory of Africana womanism, which made its debut in the mid-eighties. After presenting a historical account of evolution of Africana womanism, this volume advances the theory by further developing the concept itself, and endeavors to broaden the focus on key components of the character of the Africana womanist as a strong self-namer and self-definer whose authentic agenda dictates her family-centered persuasion regarding matters of genuine sisterhood and positive Africana male-female relationships for the ultimate survival of her people, and by extension, of the entire human race. In bringing this mission to fruition, I have engaged several literary works—Mariama Bâ's *So Long a Letter*, Buchi Emecheta's *The Joys of Motherhood*, Zora Neale Hurston's *Their Eyes Were Watching God*, Paule Marshall's *Praisesong for the Widow*, Terry McMillan's *Disappearing Acts*, Toni Morrison's *Sula* and *Beloved*, Gloria Naylor's *Mama Day*, and Sister Souljah's *No Disrespect*—as well as critics and theorists who expounded on these issues in their studies as exemplifiers of the ideal expressed in the philosophy and paradigm of Africana womanism. As an Africana womanist in today's society, I find myself positioned in the midst of chaos and confusion regarding the plight of Africana people and the ultimate challenge of creating or identifying a realistic solution to problems that serve to further devalue, demoralize, and destroy the Africana community. As stated in my earlier article "Africana Womanism and the Critical Need for Africana Theory and Thought":

131

> I cannot stress enough the critical need today for
> Africana scholars throughout the world to create our
> own paradigms and theoretical frameworks for assess-
> ing our works. We need our own Africana theorists,
> not scholars who duplicate or use theories created
> by others in analyzing Africana texts. Indeed, devel-
> oping paradigms and critical theories, which is our
> true mission, makes possible better monitoring inter-
> pretations of our works in an effort to keep them
> both authentic and accurate in order to maintain their
> originality in meaning and value. [79]

Africana womanism is just that mission realized. It could enable us to
galvanize our thoughts and ideas for the survival of our psyches and
bodies. It could enable us to leave a lasting legacy for future generations of Africana people, so that they will not be left with a void leading down the long and tiring journey of starting from scratch for
solutions to our seemingly bleak destiny.

Africana Womanist Literary Theory is more than an ideal; it is a reality. For
already, countless activists and scholars alike have come to the forefront in
seizing the opportunities this paradigm has to offer its children—the global
Africana community. It has withstood the test of debate and contempt
and has persevered through many attempts to silence and even destroy its
momentum. Through it all, it has prevailed and has victoriously rendered
an authentic workable agenda for all women of African descent, which
brings with it its male counterparts and its children. The application of literary texts to this African-centered—earlier categorized as "Black Aesthetic"
paradigm only enhances the concept via textual analysis and examples. It
validates its workability *par examples*, since literature should reflect reality.
Africana womanism, coming from that perspective, then, as aptly stated in
the Preface to *Call and Response: The Riverside Anthology of the African American
Literary Tradition* regarding that particular Black Aesthetic text, must necessarily engage in "raising important socio-political issues and the responses
to those issues either by their contemporaries or heirs in succeeding generations" (Hill xxxiii). And so it is in the concept of Africana womanism,
which neatly fits in the category of Africana literature, criticism and theory
in its authentic presentation of Africana life, history, and culture.

Epilogue

It was in 1932 that Carter G. Woodson, the father of Black historiography who is responsible for our annual Black history month celebration, came to the defense and rescue of Black women with a statement in the *Pittsburgh Courier* referencing a derogatory labeling of Black women as "Negresses." His assessment of the relationships between the sexes in the African American community indicated that there were deep-seated problems. Thus, he renounced the hypocritical efforts of black men who were in opposition to the term, "negress" while at the same time "treat[ing] our women as if they were not better than dogs." He maintained that the continued debasement and degradation of Black women will not cease until all Africana men and people stop providing ammunition to the enemy to maltreat and abuse the black woman.

The singularly nurturing construct, *Africana womanism* appears to address Woodson's concern. With its redeeming and constructive features, for over a decade and a half, this construct has introduced tools by which to foster positive relationships and promote greater understanding among the sexes in the African American community, as the first step in positive community building. Male-female relationships take center stage in this work, augmented by the demonstration of Black life through literature, which should naturally reflect life. They do so because the evidence points to the differences in the challenges confronted by black women with a history of disadvantage and oppression as opposed to whites and others. Black women were ostracized, alienated and exploited but so were their men. Lynching—a vicious, debase and dishonorable practice—was reserved not only for black men but for Black women as well. The intersection of race, class and gender in the black context, therefore, becomes central within the expanding scope of increasing marginalization and economic hardships with the advent of globalization.

Any serious scholar in the academy knows that methodologies come and go. However, the application of the Africana Womanist theory shows that its existence will be long-term. It demonstrates overpowering mission to empower those seeking an effective change agent in the social reconstruction of male-female relationships in the black community. Black male-female relationships, undoubtedly the foundation for building a strong allegiance against racial oppression, are a force to reckon with. Besides deconstructing the myths pertaining to relationships among Black men and women, Africana womanism demystifies those anxieties and fears Black women have to promote inclusiveness and to push for a better stake at a society that promises every other race but them a chance at the American dream. An analysis of the paradigm and its eighteen steps reveals that Hudson-Weems' treatise is explicitly related to the Black woman's disadvantaged historical and cultural experience strongly rooted in this society, which she presents through her interpretation of key literary texts. The existence of Africana people in a dominant patriarchal system of power brokering often excludes them and puts Black women even at a double disadvantage.

A perfect example of this is represented in the saga of Sister Souljah, a celebrated female rap artist in pop culture whose voice enriches the Africana womanist agenda, tells our story more convincingly than any other. Through introspection, she engages in autobiographical discourse that shapes her life and the lives of her family. Collectively theirs was a life of pain and economic tribulation, a life of challenges in a single-parent, female-headed household on welfare dependency, and a life that is not unique to her and to the millions of black families disproportionately represented on the welfare rolls with little hope for the future. The complementarities in the analysis and dissection of issues in family and male-female relationships make this writer a disciple in the Africana womanist tradition. Educated, resolute, self-assured and positively opinionated, she articulates a road map for blacks. She realizes that education is a good thing but she is also aware that education designed to reinforce stereotypes, reproduce injustice and promote unethical behavior is unacceptable. The lessons shared by Sister Souljah in her autobiography, *No Disrespect*, are pointed. She cuts across cultural boundaries to address traditional sexual inequity and explores variables of race, class and gender and the complexities of a hateful society that puts men against women and race against race. Her work strikes a match with the Africana womanist paradigm and spells out the dynamics of institutionalized racism without apology. She shares the hope of minimizing poverty of blacks and reclaiming a life of prosperity and dignity that was more characteristic of Africanans before slavery and colonialism. She references the fact that social, spiritual and political relations must coincide with a strong economic position to alleviate pain and suffering in our neighborhoods.

While her vision for a holistic, self-sustaining community is not new to Black people, her story validates the Africana womanist position and provides new directions and a basis for continuing the dialogue dedicated to improving male-female relationships and the quality of Black life worldwide. To be sure, Blacks may more expediently help to create positive global communities, which is the ultimate vision for the true Africana womanist.

Daphne Ntiri-Quenum, Ph.D.
Director of the Office of Adult & Lifelong Learning Research
Associate Professor Social Sciences & Interdisciplinary Studies
Wayne State University

Afterword

Clearly, the past twenty years have been the most fruitful intellectual times of the African American community, because scholars have produced some of the most compelling works in history. To a great extent it has been because of the theoretical reach of enlightened African women and men scholars who have challenged the boundaries of racist scholarship to cross over into an intellectual field of wonder. Clenora Hudson-Weems is just such a scholar as she demonstrates in *Africana Womanist Literary Theory*, a brilliant sequel to her first book on the subject, *Africana Womanism: Reclaiming Ourselves* (1993). A pioneer in explaining and promoting the role, responsibility, dignity, and capacity of Africana women without the destructive overtones often found in the writings of other women, Hudson-Weems is certainly in the top class of scholars dealing with these important issues.

What this book demonstrates is that African American Studies scholars will continue to create new formations and approaches to the understanding of literary texts. There could be nothing more profound than the appreciation of a literary tradition rooted in the agency of African people. This, relatively, is a new avenue of locating a text, arriving at a new destination, one that will help to liberate the minds of readers.

Hudson-Weems' intellectual ideas will have a multiplier effect on the writing of scholars who seek to interpret the work of African women writers. She has established that Africana womanism is a viable and effective method of ascertaining the purpose, role, and direction of literature written by or about Africana people.

Every author who has written in this tradition has sought to reorient our thinking away from the power relationships established for the interests of white art, aesthetics, and literature. One could read such narrowly defined artistic work with almost no reference to the broad African tradition of critical scholarship. One of the conditions of weakness in a society of racial domination is to have even one's art defined by the dominant culture. In this regard the work becomes either good or bad, depending upon the relationship it bears to the domination.

My own purpose in this afterword is to speak to those values that

137

say the Africana woman, as defined by Hudson-Weems, has been a relatively quiet voice but will be a quiet voice no longer. Whether one is defining literary essences or creating visions of the future, nothing will be as significant as the need for us to continue to advance the science and art of discovering, as these authors have discovered the multiplicity of complex voices that sing a song of Africana woman unity.

The fact of the matter is that Africana womanism is a response to the need for collective definition and the re-creation of the authentic agenda that is the birthright of every living person. In order to make this shift to authenticity, Hudson-Weems has called us back to the earliest days of African cultural history. In this antiquity she has discovered the sources of so much commonality in the African world that there is no question that Africana womanism has a distinct and different approach to relationships than, say, feminism. It is the African woman's own voice emerging from the debris of a vast cultural wasteland in the Western world. Having been the victims of so much brutality in the West, the African woman, in all of her guises, comes now to the forefront of the struggle for centeredness.

Perhaps one of the most important challenges facing Africana womanism, much like challenges we have seen in other Afrocentric ventures, is keeping clever writers from siphoning off ideas and then claiming that those ideas really belong to feminism or to some other Western construction. What the African community has come to applaud is the clarity with which Hudson-Weems speaks about African women. She has often pointed out, as she does in this volume, that many women authors try to suggest that the self-definition, self-determination, and centering that she has articulated is really a part of some feminist movement. In fact, what has usually happened is that those writers have found the Afrocentric ideas and concepts developed in Hudson-Weems' Africana womanism significant and, therefore, have sought to appropriate them without proper attribution. I believe that this exists because they do not want to admit that their concepts were first conceived in the writings of the Africana womanist school. This book, to be certain, is critical to a full understanding of the substantive contributions of women scholars to our total liberation. It is true, as Ama Mazama has observed, that Africana womanism seeks to correct the total inadequacy of feminism to appreciate the reality of African women. In fact, what Hudson-Weems demonstrates is that no transformation can take place without a rethinking of the way Africana women have been viewed and view themselves in the Western world.

Molefi Kete Asante,* Ph.D.
Professor of African American Studies
Temple University

*Molefi Kete Asante coined the term *Afrocentricity*.

Index

Mompati, Ruth 38, 42, 54

Moore, Richard B. xix, 52

Mootry, Maria K. 15

Morrison, Toni ii, viii, xvi, xxii-xxiii, 1, 9, 18, 37, 49, 62, 65, 70-72, 74, 105, 115-116, 118-119, 121-122, 126-131

mothering xx, 18, 33, 53, 59

movie viii, , 127-130

Mr. Right 69, 104

N

name xviii-xix, xxi, 5-7, 12, 19-21, 28, 35, 39, 42, 47, 50, 109-110, 118, 122, 129

Nation's first xxiii

National Council for Black Studies xi, 2, 3, 12

National Women's Studies Association 2

Naylor, Gloria 17, 69, 131

Neimah ix

Newson-Horst, Adele S. 17

New York Times Magazine 9

Nigeria xvii-xviii, xxii, 1, 11-12, 48

nigger 120

No Disrespect viii, xxii, 99, 101, 131, 134

Nommo vii, xii, xix, xxi, 1, 6-7, 18

NOW 25

Ntiri-Quenum, Daphne viii, 135

nurturing xvi, xviii, xx, 18, 25, 33, 52, 53, 59, 67, 71, 74, 95, 118, 126, 133

P

paradigm xii, xviii-xx, xxii, 1-3, 5, 7-8, 10-11, 16-19, 27-28,

35, 45, 50, 60, 68, 83, 91, 93, 131-132, 134

Parks, Rosa 8, 46-47, 52, 80

patriarchal 19, 28, 38, 42, 81, 85-87, 134

Paul D xxiii, 37, 116, 118-123, 128-129

politics 9, 16, 19-20, 29, 86, 88

Polygamy xv, 58, 80

Praisesong for the Widow xxii, 60, 131

prioritize 29, 96

Procrustean xxi, 10

proud vii, xvii, xxii, 51, 54, 57, 76

R

race empowerment xxiii, 19, 51-52, 57, 63, 82

racism xiii, xxiii, 2, 17, 19, 25, 27, 29-31, 38-39, 43-44, 48, 52, 54-55, 67, 80-81, 87, 89, 93, 96-97, 99-101, 105, 112, 115, 119, 134

recognized xx, 13, 18, 20

Reed, Pamela Yaa Asantewaa vii, xviii, 17

relationships xxiii, 70, 73-74, 80, 83-84, 88-90, 92, 96-97, 99-100, 104, 106-107, 111, 133-134, 137-138

respected xx, 15, 18, 32, 69, 105

respectful of elders xx, 18, 90, 118

Richards, Beah 128

S

Samuels, Wilfred D. ii, 37, 62, 105, 116-117, 119, 121-122, 126, 130